Letters That Have Helped Me

WILLIAM Q. JUDGE

Letters That Have Helped Me

Compiled by
JASPER NIEMAND

THEOSOPHICAL UNIVERSITY PRESS
PASADENA, CALIFORNIA

THEOSOPHICAL UNIVERSITY PRESS
PASADENA, CALIFORNIA 91109
1981

These LETTERS originally appeared in *The Path*, December 1888 to March 1890. W. Q. Judge first published them in book form in 1891, and this present edition is a verbatim reprint of that original.

The paper in this book meets the standards for permanence and durability of the Council on Library Resources.

Library of Congress Catalog Card Number 81-52614
Hardcover ISBN 0-911500-41-3
Softcover ISBN 0-911500-42-1

MANUFACTURED IN THE UNITED STATES OF AMERICA

To
Z. L. Z.
the Greatest of
the Exiles, and Friend
of all Creatures; from his
Younger Brother, the Compiler.

JASPER NIEMAND
1891

Preface

"Seeking for freedom I go to that God who is the light of his own thoughts. A man who knows him truly passes over death; there is no other path to go." — *Upanishads*

In the *Path* for May, 1887, we find these words:
"We need a literature, not solely for highly intellectual persons, but of a more simple character, which attempts to appeal to ordinary common-sense minds who are really fainting for such moral and mental assistance as is not reached by the more pretentious works."

The experience of one student is, on the whole, the experience of all. Details differ, however. Some are made more instantly rich than others: they are those who put forth more vigorous and generous effort; or they have a Karmic store which brings aid. What Theosophists know as Karma, or the law of spiritual action and reaction, decided this, as it works on all the planes, physical, moral, mental, psychical, and spiritual alike. Our Karma may be worked out on any one of these planes when our life is chiefly concentrated upon it, no matter upon what other plane any special initiative impulse or branch of it originated.

The writer, when first he became a theosophical student, had the aid of an advanced occultist in his studies. This friend sent him, among others, the letters which, in the hope that they may assist others as they have the original recipient, are here published. They are not exhaustive treatises; they are hints given by one who knew that the first need of a student is to learn *how to think*. The true direction is pointed out, and the student is left to clarify his own perceptions, to draw upon and enlarge his own intuitions, and to develop, as every created thing must at last develop, by his own inward exertions. Such students have passed the point where their external environment can affect their growth favorably. They may learn from it, but the time has also come to resist it and turn to the internal adjustment to higher relations only.

The brevity of these letters should not mislead the reader. Every statement in them is a statement of law. They point to causes of which life is an effect; that life arising from the action of Spirit in Nature, and which we must understand as it is manifested within us before we can advance on the Path. There is a scientific meaning within all these devotional or ethical injunctions, for the Wisdom-Religion never relaxes her hold upon Science or attempts to dissever an effect from its cause. Most of these admonitions have their base in the constitution of the Archaeus, or World-Soul, and the correlation of its energies; others, still, adhere in the Eternal.

No less should the reader guard himself against a slight estimate arising from the exquisite modesty of Z. An occultist is never so truly a man of power as when he has wholly learned and exhibits this truth:

"And the power the disciple shall desire is that which shall make him appear as nothing *in the eyes of men.*"

The inner eye, *the power of seeing*, looks deeper into the source of a man's knowledge and takes it at its true value. Those men who are sharers in the Divine, whose first office is to give, are often protected from the demands and curiosity of the careless by a simple exterior which deceives the worldly sense. Some men are great because of the Power which stands behind them, the divine energies which flow through them;

they are great through having learned how to receive this celestial influx from higher spheres of Being; they are the appointed ministrants, the true servitors of the Law and pupils of Masters whose office is humanitarian and universal.

Such aid is never volunteered; it follows the Karmic behest, and, when given, leaves the student free to follow it or not, as his intuitions may direct. There is not a shadow or vestige of *authority* in the matter, as the world understands the word *authority*. Those who travel the unknown way send messages back, and he who can receives them. Only a few of the first steps are here recorded and the first impediments surmounted. No hints of magic lore are to be found; no formulas of creed or occult powers; the questions of an awakening soul are answered, and the pilgrim is shown where lies the entrance to the Path. The world at large seeks the facts of occult science, but the student who has resolved to attain desires to find the true road. What may seem to others as mere ethics is to him practical instruction, for as he follows it he soon perceives its relation to facts and laws which he is enabled to verify, and what seemed to him the language of devotion merely, is found to be that of science; but the science is spiritual, for the Great Cause is pure Spirit.

Many students must at some time stand where the writer then stood, at the beginning of the way. For all these this correspondence is made public, and they are urged to look within the printed words for their imperishable meaning. They may be cheered to find the footprints of a comrade upon the rugged Path, above which the light of Truth ever shines. Yet even this light is not always a clear splendor. It may seem "in the daytime a cloud, and by night a pillar of fire." We must question every external aspect, even that of Faith itself, for the secret and germ of things lies at their core. Let us purify even our Faith; let us seek Truth herself, and not our preconceptions of Truth. In her mirror we shall never see our own familiar face: that which we see is still ourselves, because our real self is truth.

As the Theosophical movement gathers new momentum, fresh recruits may be aided by those letters which so greatly sustained me, or encouraged by some co-partnership of thought, and that, too, in the real issue confronting them. We first take this issue to be the acquirement of occult knowledge. Soon we find that the meaning of all really informed occult writers eludes us. We find that books only serve to remind us of what we knew in the long past, perhaps when "journeying with Deity," and the echoes awakened within us are so faint that they are rarely to be caught. Whether we study philosophies, metaphysics, physics, ethics, harmony, astrology, natural sciences, astralism, magnetism, or what not, we meet with endless contradiction and differentiation; we forever require to strike the balance of our own intuition. We discover that the final word has not yet been *written down* upon any of the higher subjects (unless it be on mathematics, and scarcely on that), and that all our learning is but a finger-post to that supreme knowledge of Truth which is only found and closely guarded within the human heart. Thrown back upon our inner perceptions for continual readjustment, on every side of experience this warning confronts us: *Stand ready to abandon all thou hast learned!* Not knowing the one center, we cannot thoroughly know any sub-center. The cause unknown, effects mislead us. Then we turn to that mysterious center whereby the One is manifest in man, and we begin the study of the heart, both in itself and in the life it has instituted about us.

To be put into more direct communication with the world of cause is now the student's most pressing need. One thing alone prevents this — himself. He is of such gross fibre that he cannot be "porous to thought, bibulous of the sea of light." To the refinement and dispersal of this lower self — of the man he now takes himself to be — he then directs his will. Each man has a different mode of doing this, but each who advances at all finds that with every new period of his inner life a new self rises before him. Looking back over a group of weeks or months, he is amazed to see what manner of man he was then, and smiles that pitying smile which we bestow upon the faded letters of our youth.

Yet some there be who ossify there in their rut; let them struggle mightily to break up the mass which has resisted all environment, all change, all the conditions of progressive life. They have done for themselves what the enemy strives to do for others; they are the rock in their own path.

What our Eastern brothers call "the sheaths of the heart" fall away one by one; when the last bursts open there is a silence, the silence of the mystic death. But "the dead shall arise," and from that death springs up the first tender growth of eternal life.

Up to this point we shall not travel in the ensuing pages. Yet having realized the real issue so forcibly that his whole strength was at the start directed towards self-knowledge and the right use of Thought, the writer offers a part of his first instructions to those of his comrades who, single-hearted and of royal Faith, hold Truth to be dearer than all material life and seek it on the hidden way. There is no tie in the universe equal to that which binds such comrades together. It has been forged in the fires of unspeakable anguish; it has been rivetted by a dauntless purpose and a unique, because Divine, Love. The fierce hatred of seen and unseen worlds cannot tamper with it so long as a man remains true to himself, for this larger life is himself, and as he grows towards it his self-imposed fetters fall away and he stands, at last, a free soul, in the celestial Light which is Freedom itself, obedient only to the Law of its own divine Being. To reach it, let us obey the law of our own Being, for, truly, *Being is One.*

My comrades, wherever you are, I salute you.

JASPER NIEMAND, F. T. S.

Letters That Have Helped Me

I

My Dear Jasper:

Now let me elevate a signal. Do not think much of me, please. Think kindly of me; but oh, my friend, direct your thoughts to the Eternal Truth. I am, like you, struggling on the road. Perhaps a veil might in an instant fall down from your spirit, and you would be long ahead of us all. The reason you have had help is that in other lives you gave it to others. In every effort you made to lighten another mind and open it to Truth, you were helped yourself. Those pearls you found for another and gave to him, you really retained for yourself in the act of benevolence. For when one lives thus to help others, he is thereby putting in practice the rule to try and "kill out all sense of separateness," and thus gets little by little in possession of the true light.

Never lose, then, that attitude of mind. Hold fast in silence to all that is your own, for you will need it in the fight; but never, *never* desire to get knowledge or power for any other purpose than to give it on the altar, for thus alone can it be saved to you.

So many are there around me who are ardent desirers and seekers, devotees; but they are doing it because the possession seems valuable. Perhaps I see in you — I hope I mistake not — a pure desire to seek Knowledge for its own sake, and that all others may be benefitted. So I would point out to you the only royal road, the one vehicle. Do all those acts, physical, mental, moral, for the reason that they must be done, instantly resigning all interest in them, offering them up upon the altar. What altar? Why, the great spiritual altar, which is, if one desires it, in the heart. Yet still use earthly discrimination, prudence, and wisdom.

It is not that you must rush madly or boldly out *to do, to do*. Do what you find to do. Desire ardently to do it, and even when you shall not have succeeded in carrying anything out but some small duties, some words of warning, your strong desire will strike like Vulcan upon other hearts in the world, and suddenly you will find that done which you had longed to be the doer of. Then rejoice that another had been so fortunate as to make such a meritorious Karma. Thus, like the rivers running into the unswelling, passive ocean, will your desires enter into your heart.

I find all your remarks just; and besides, there seems to be a real spirit behind them. Do not fear nor fail because you feel dark and heavy. The very rage you feel will break the shrine that covers the mystery after a while. No one can really help you. No one can open your doors. You locked them up, and only you can open them. When you open any door, beyond it you find others standing there who had passed you long ago, but now, unable to proceed, they are there waiting; others are there waiting for you. Then you come, and, opening a door, those waiting disciples perhaps may pass on; thus on and on. What a privilege this, to reflect that we may perhaps be able to help those who seemed greater than ourselves!

O, what a groan Nature gives to see the heavy Karma which man has piled upon himself and all the creatures of the three worlds! That deep sigh pierces through my heart. How can the load be lifted? Am I to stand for myself, while the few strong hands of Blessed Masters and Their friends hold back the awful cloud? Such a vow I registered ages ago to help them, and I must. Would to great Karma I could do more! And you! do what you can.

Place your only faith, reliance, and trust on Karma.

Z.

II

MY DEAR BROTHER:

Your last long letter came duly to hand and has been read with much pleasure. It is quite rare to find one willing to enter this movement on the basis you have laid down for yourself, and my previous letter was written in order to see what your attitude really was, and also because I then felt from your writing that you were really in earnest. And before yours of today, I fell to thinking about you and wondering whether a future of power, a brilliancy of knowledge, was not your aspiration, and what effect certain occurrences would have upon that.

Judge, then, my pleasure in reading your words exactly answering my mental inquiries of yesterday and placing you in the right position.

It is true, we must aspire ardently, and blessed is the one who, after the first aspiration, is wise enough to see the Truth.

Three qualities forever encompass us: *Satwa* (truth and stability), *Rajas* (action, war, aspiration, ambition), *Tamas* (indifference, ignorance, darkness).

None may be ignored. So the path lies from Tamas, up through war, ambition, and aspiration, to Satwa, or truth and stability. We are now in Rajasika regions, sometimes lifting our fingers up to the hem of the garment of Satwa, ever aspiring, ever trying to purify our thoughts and free ourselves from the attachment to action and objects. So, of course, the ardent student naturally aspires for power. This is wise. But he must soon begin to see what he must do for real progress. For continual aspiration for power merely is sure to sow for us the giant weed of self, which is the giant spoken of in *Light on the Path.*

As to the Theosophical Society, all should be admitted, for we can refuse *no one*. If this is a Universal Brotherhood, we can make no distinctions; but we can put ourselves right in the beginning by seeing that people do not enter with mistaken notions of what we have. And yet with all our precautions, how often we find persons who are not really sincere themselves judging us by their standard, unbelieving in our sincerity. They enter; they find that each must study for himself and that no guides are told off to reach one; then they are disgusted. They forget that "the kingdom of heaven must be taken by violence." We have also had to suffer from our friends. People who have joined us in secret like Nicodemus; they have stood idly by, waiting for the Cause to get strong or to get fashionable, and leaving all the hard fighting to be done by a few earnest men who defied the hosts of Materialism and of Conventionality. Had they spoken for their Cause, more earnest people would long ago have heard of the movement, instead of being kept away until now, like yourself, for want of knowledge that it existed.

You will find that other members care for nothing but Theosophy, and are yet forced by circumstances to work in other fields as well. What moments they have left are devoted to the Cause, and in consequence they have no unoccupied hours; each moment, day and evening, is filled up, and therefore they are happy. Yet they are unhappy that they cannot give their entire working time to the Cause in which some have been from the beginning. They feel, like Claude St. Martin, a burning desire within them to get these truths to the ears of all men. They are truths, and you are in the right path. In America it is as easy to find the Light of Lights as in India, but all around you are those who do not know these things, who never heard of them, and yet many of our fellow members are only anxious to study for their own benefit. Sometimes, if it were not for my reliance on those Great Beings who beckon me ever on, I would faint, and, leaving these people to themselves, rush off into the forest. So many people like Theosophy, and yet they at once wish to make it select and of high tone. It is for all men. It is for the common people, who are ever with us. Others, again, come in and wait like young birds for food to be put into them: they *will not think*, and ages must pass before they will progress.

You misunderstood a little the words "Do not think much of me." Underline "*much*," but not "think." You will please think all the thoughts you will of me, but do not place me on any pinnacle: that's all I meant.

A constant endeavor towards perfecting the mere mortal machine is folly. Thereby we sometimes fail to live up to our own intuitions. This habit goes on for some time, but will get weaker as other senses (inner ones) begin to appear. Yet know the new fully before being off with the old.

Inasmuch as we learn almost solely from each other — as we are all here for each other — the question of the effect of affinities upon our acts and thoughts is enormous and wide. It anon saves us, and anon damns. For we may meet in our lives a person who has a remarkable effect, either for good or ill, because of the affinities engendered in past lives. And now our eyes are open, we act today for the future.

That you may pass beyond the sea of darkness, I offer you my life and help. **Z.**

III

SAY, Brother Jasper, are you tired? I am. Not tired of fate or of the great "Leaders of the World," but with all these people who gape and gape and are (excuse me) so Americanly "independent," as if men were ever independent of each other.

You ask about the "moment of choice." It is made up of all moments. It is not in space or time, but is the aggregation of those moments flying by us each instant. It is referred to in *Esoteric Buddhism* as a period not yet arrived for the race, when it will as a whole be compelled to make choice for good or evil. But any single individual can bring on the period for himself. When it will or has come, the uninstructed cannot tell. For the student of occultism it may come in the next instant, or it may come one hundred lives after. But it cannot come this instant unless all the previous lives have led up to it. Yet as regards the student, even if it be presented to him and he refuse, he will be brought to the choice in future existences, with the whole body of his race. Race influences are insidious and powerful. For instance, my race has its peculiarities deeply seated and inherited from an extraordinary past. I must be under their influence in this body as a necessary part of my experience. In another life I might have been a prosaic Hottentot, or an Englishman, and in a succeeding one I might be under the influence of other race peculiarities. Those influences are, then, guiding me every moment, and each thought I have adds to them now, for either my own future use or for some other person who will come under the power of part of the force generated now by me.

As to the sub-conscious mind. It is difficult to explain. I find constantly that I have ideas that internally I thoroughly understand, and yet can find no language for them. Call it sub-conscious if you like. It is there and can be affected; indeed, it is affected every moment. It is a nearness to the universal mind. So if I desire to influence — say your mind — I do not formulate your sub-conscious plane, but firmly and kindly think of you and think of the subject I wish you to think of. This must reach you. If I am selfish, then it has more difficulty to get there; but if it be brotherly, then it gets there more easily, being in harmony with the universal mind and the Law. The Psychical Society speaks of it, and says that the influence "emerges into the lower mind" by one or more of the channels. But they do not know what those "channels" are, or even if they do exist. In fact, the whole subject of mind is only faintly understood in the West. They say "mind," meaning the vast range and departments of that which they call mind, whereas there must be a need for the names of those departments. When the true ideas are grasped, the names will follow. Meanwhile we must be satisfied with "mind" as including the whole thing. But it does not. Certainly it is not ordinary mental motion — ratiocination — to grasp in an instant a whole subject, premises and conclusions, without stopping to reason. It cannot be called a *picture*, for with some it comes as an idea, and not as a picture. Memory. What is that? Is it brain-impression; or similarity of vibration, recognized upon being repeated and then producing a picture? If so, then the power to recognize the vibration as the same as before is separate from the matter which vibrates. And if the power inhere in the brain cells, how is it possible, when we know they are constantly being changed? Yet memory is perfect, no matter what happens. That it is above brain is clear, because a man may be killed by having his brain blown to atoms, and yet his "shell" can give all the incidents of his life, and they are not taken from the brain, for that is dead. Where, then, is the sub-conscious mind? And where are the channels, and how are they connected? I think through the heart, and that the heart is the key to it all, and that the brain is only the servant of the heart,* for remember that there is in it the "small dwarf who sits at the centre." Think it out on that line now for yourself — or any other line that you may choose, but *think*. As ever, Z.

IV

DEAR SIR AND BROTHER:

In cogitating lately I thought of you in respect to some of my own thoughts. I was reading a book and looking around within myself to see how I could enlarge my idea of brotherhood. Practice in benevolence will not give it its full growth. I had to find some means of reaching further, and struck on this, which is as old as old age.

I am not separate from anything. "I am that which is." That is, I am Brahma, and Brahma is everything. But being in an illusionary world, I am surrounded by certain appearances that seem to make me separate. So I will proceed to

---

*Not the physical heart, but the real centre of life in man.
— J. N.

mentally state and accept that I am all these illusions. I am my friends, — and then I went to them in general and in particular. I am my enemies; then I felt them all. I am the poor and the wicked; I am the ignorant. Those moments of intellectual gloom are the moments when I am influenced by those ignorant ones who are myself. All this in my nation. But there are many nations, and to those I go in mind; I feel and I am them all, with what they hold of superstition or of wisdom or evil. All, all is myself. Unwisely, I was then about to stop, but the whole is Brahma, so I went to the Devas and Asuras:* the elemental world, that too is myself. After pursuing this course awhile I found it easier to return to a contemplation of all men as myself. It is a good method and ought to be pursued, for it is a step toward getting into contemplation of the All. I tried last night to reach up to Brahma, but darkness is about his pavilion.

Now what does all this insanity sound like? I'll tell you what: if it were not for this insanity I would go insane. But shall I not take heart, even when a dear friend deserts me and stabs me deep, when I know that he is myself?

NAMASTAE!   Z.

I found the above letter still more valuable when I remembered that Brahma is "the universal expansive force of Nature" — from *Brih*, to expand; and so stated in an article by H. P. Blavatsky in *Five Years of Theosophy*. In the *Dhammapada* we are told to think ourselves to be the sun and stars, the wet and dry, heat and cold; in short, to feel all experience, for we can live all out in the mind.

J. N.

*Gods and demons. — J. N.

V

DEAR JASPER:

I wish I could answer your letter as you ought to have it done. But I feel my inability. However, our duty is to never consider our ability, but to do what comes to be done in whatever way we can, no matter how inadequate the work appears to others. When we stop to consider our weakness, we think, by comparison, of how another would do it. Our *only right is in the act itself.* The consequences are in the great Brahm. So I will just say what comes.

I feel the sadness in your letter, but know that you will rebound from that. Do not let the sadness of knowledge create despair; that sadness is less than the joy of Truth. Abstract Truth, even, has necessarily in it all the mercy there is in the whole. Its sternness is only a reflection from our own imperfections, which make us recognize the stern aspect alone. We are not the only ones to suffer upon the Path. Like ourselves, Masters have wept, though They do not now weep. One of them wrote some years ago: "Do you suppose we have not passed through many times worse trials than you now think you are in?" The Master often seems to reject and to hide his (spiritual) face, in order that the disciple may try. On the doors and walls of the temple the word "TRY" is written. ("The Brothers" is a better designation than Mahâtmas or Masters.)

Along the path of the true student is sadness, but also there is great joy and hope. Sadness comes from a more just appreciation of the difficulties in one's way, and of the great wickedness of the individual and collective heart of man. But look at the great fountain of hope and of joy in the consideration that the Brothers exist, that They were men too; They had to fight the fight; They triumphed, and

They work for those left after Them. Then beyond Them are "the Fathers," that is, the spirits of "just men made perfect," those Who lived and worked for humanity ages ago and Who are now out of our sphere, but Who nevertheless still influence us in that Their spiritual forces flow down upon this earth for all pure souls. Their immediate influence is felt by Masters, and by us through the latter.

Now, as you say, it is all Faith; but what is Faith? It is the intuitional feeling — "*that is true*." So formulate to yourself certain things as true that you feel to be true, and then increase your faith in them.

Don't be anxious. Don't get "maddened." Because in the fact that you are "maddened" (of course in the metaphorical sense) is found the proof that you are anxious. In a worldly sense it is perhaps well to be anxious about a highly important matter, but in occultism it is different, for the Law takes no account of our projects and objects, or our desire to be ahead or behind. So, if we are anxious, we raise a barrier against progress, by perturbation and straining harshly. You wrote to B. that what is his, is his. Then the converse is true; what is not, is not. Why don't you take your own medicine?

Yours,   Z.

VI

DEAR JASPER:

It is a great advance that you hear the bells, which few hear, and evidence that you are where you can hear them; that is a great deal indeed. Do not look for the voice of the bells, but regard the *ideas* which thereupon come into the head, and apply to them the touchstone of your own Soul, just as you advised B. The fact that you feel "dead" is something you should not worry about. It is likely that you are under the operation of a law which prevails in nature, that you will find referred to in an article in *Path* Magazine for April, '86, page 14. It is that the soul goes to a new place or new surroundings and becomes silent there awhile — what you call "dead" — and draws strength there, begins to get accustomed to its new surroundings, after which it begins to move about. This is seen in ordinary life in the bashfulness of a boy. That is, the bashfulness is the shyness felt in new surroundings, and is just what happens when the soul goes to a new place or into new surroundings. There can be no loss or detriment to our efforts. Every aspiration higher brightens up the road connecting the higher and lower self. No doubt of that. It is not *what* is done, but the spirit in which the least thing is done that is counted. Hear the word of the Master.

"He who does the best he knows how and that he can do, does enough for us."

The mere fact that a man appreciates these truths and feels these aspirations is proof that he is on the right road. It is well to tread it *now*. We will not always live. Death must come. How much better, then, to embrace death while thus at work than to swerve off only to be brought up with suddenness in after lives. Immediate rebirth is for those who are always working with their hearts on Master's work and free from self interest.

The one Spirit is in all, is the property of each, therefore It is always there, always with us, and, by reflecting on that, little room is left for sorrow or delusion. If we believe that the soul of all is measured by the whole of Time and not by a part, then we care not for these moments which relate alone to our body. If we live in our hearts we soon prove that space and time exist not. Nothing foreign to Master enters there; our faults are not there. The heart reaches Him always, and no doubt He replies. He does I know. He helps us while He leaves us to ourselves. He needs not to stoop to see our devotion, for that is of a supernal quality and reaches anywhere.

No, I do not say nor have I said that you ought to do something other than you do. We each do what we can. None of us can be the judge of any creature existing; so I do not judge you in the least respect. Your life may in the great sum total be greater than any life I ever led or that any one has led. Whether you are in America, Europe, or India makes no difference. This is seeking conditions. I have come to understand that Masters themselves must have worked themselves up out of much worse conditions than we are in. No matter where we are, the same spirit pervades all and is accessible. What need, then, to change places? We do not change ourselves by moving the body to another *locus*. We only put it under a different influence. And in order to change we must have got to dislike the place we moved from. That is *attachment by opposites*, and that will produce detriment, as does all that disturbs the equilibrium of the soul. You know the same result is produced by two exact opposites, and thus extremes meet.

That hot flame you speak of is one of the experiences, as are also the sounds. There are so many, many of these things. Often they result from extreme tension or vibration in the aura of an aspirant of pure devotion. They are himself, and he should be on his guard against taking them for wonders. Often they are "apparitions of Brahm." They are like new lights and sights to a mariner on an unfamiliar coast. They will go on, or alter, or stop. You are only to carefully note them, and "do not exhibit wonder nor form association."

I cannot say more. All help you extend to any other soul is help to yourself. It is our duty to help all, and we must begin on those nearest to us, for to run abroad to souls we might possibly help we again forsake our present duty. It is better to die in our own duty, however mean, than to try another one. So lift your head and look around upon the hulks of past imagined faults. They were means and teachers. Cast all doubt, all fear, all regret aside, and freely take of truth what you may contain right on every step. It will thus be well. Eternal Truth is one and indivisible, and we may get from the Fathers (Pitris) flashes now and then of what is true.

Words are things. With me and in fact. Upon the lower plane of social intercourse they are things, but soulless and dead because that convention in which they have their birth has made abortions of them. But when we step away from that conventionality they become alive in proportion to the reality of the thought — and its purity — that is behind them. So in communication between two students they are things, and those students must be careful that the ground of intercourse is fully understood. Let us use with care those living messengers called words.

Where I see you mistaken I will speak, to warn my Brother who temporarily knows not. For did I not call on the bugle, perhaps other things might switch him off to where perhaps for the time he would be pleased, but would again be sorry, and then when his mistake was plain he would justly sigh to me across dark centuries of separation that I had been false to my duty of warning.

As ever, Z.

The new plane to which the soul may go, referred to in this letter, is the astral plane. It is the plane next above the material one, and consists of a subtile order of matter. When a student turns his attention to the higher life and desires intensely to find the way, his soul has begun to awaken and to speak. It has heard the voice of the spirit. Then the inner senses begin to unfold, at first ever so gently, so tenderly, we scarce hear their report. But the soul has then turned its attention to the astral plane, that being the next one to be learned on the way upward; its energy is transferred from the material plane to this one, and we have an influx of many confused dreams and strange experiences, awake and asleep. These may or may not continue; all depends upon the individual soul and upon Karma. It is a most confusing plane, and, generally speaking, we may say that those students are more fortunate who make a marked degree of progress in spiritual things without having any conscious experience of the astral plane. For then they can later on learn it *from above*, instead of from below, and with far less danger to themselves. The whole must be known, but we may progress in various ways, even by discontinuous degrees, only then we must go back later on, to what we passed by. Such a going back does not imply detriment or loss of degree, for such cannot be lost when once gained in reality.

With regard to the astral plane's being a more subtile order of matter, this truth is often denied by clairvoyants and untrained seers. They do not distinguish between the psychic senses and the spiritual. They can see through gross matter, such as a wall, the human body, and so forth, as if it were glass, but they cannot see through astral substance, and hence they believe its forms and all the pictures and shapes in the astral light to be real. Only the adept sees through these illusions, which are far more powerful because composed of a subtile order of matter: subtile energies, fine forces have a highly increased rate of power over grosser ones. The adept has at his command the rate of vibration which dispels them or drives them asunder. In speaking of the astral plane, I mean the lower soul plane, and not that higher and purified quality which the author of *Light on the Path* calls the "divine astral."

By anxiety we exert the constrictive power of egoism, which densifies and perturbs our magnetic sphere, rendering us less permeable to the efflux from above.   J. N.

VII

DEAR JASPER:

I have your letter, Comrade, in which you say how much you wish there were some Adepts sent to the United States to help all true students. Yet you know well They do not need to come here in person, in order to help. By going carefully over your letter there appears to be the possibility of the seed of doubt in your heart as to the wise ordering of all things, for all are under the Law, and Masters first of all. Mind, I only say the *"possibility of the seed of doubt."* For I judge from my own experience. Well do I remember when I thought as you say, how much better 'twould be if some one were there.

If that is allowed to remain it will metamorphose itself into a seed and afterward a plant of doubt. Cast it right out! It does not now show as a seed of doubt, but it will be a case of metamorphosis, and the change would be so great as to deceive you into thinking it were never from the same root. The best stand to take is that it is all right as it is now, and when the time comes for it to be better it will be so. Meanwhile we have a duty to see that we do all we can *in our own place* as we see best, undisturbed and undismayed by aught.

How much I have in years gone away said and thought those very words of yours and to no profit! Why do you care what becomes of a million human beings? Are not millions going to death daily with no one to tell them of all this? But did you suppose that all this was not provided for? "And heavenly death itself is also well provided for." Now, then, you and I must learn to look on the deaths or the famishing of millions of beings with unfaltering heart. Else we had better give it all up now. Consider that at this moment are so many persons in various far distant places who cannot ever hear these truths. Do you grieve for them? Do you realize their state? No; you realize only partially the same thing among those with whom it was your present lot to be born — I mean the nation. Do you want to do more than your best? Do you covet the work of another? No; you do not. You will sit calmly where you are, then, and, with an unaffected heart, picture to yourself the moral and physical deaths and famines which are now without the possibility of prevention or amelioration. Your faith will know that *all* is provided for.

I do not say that you must attain to that calm *now* or give up seeking the Way; but I do say that you must admit that such an attainment must be absolutely tried for. For of such is the trial, and why should we care? *We must some day be able to stand any shock*, and to get ready for that time we must be now triumphant over some smaller things. Among others is the very position you and I are now in; that is, standing our ground and feeling ourselves so much and so awfully alone. But we know that They have left us a commandment. That we keep, although now and then objects, senses, men, and time conspire to show us that Masters laugh at us. It is all a delusion. It is only one consequence of our past Karma now burning itself out before our eyes. The whole phantasmagoria is only a picture thrown up against the Screen of Time by the mighty magic of Prakriti (Nature). But you and I are superior to Nature. Why, then, mind these pictures? Part of that very screen, however, being our own mortal bodies, we can't help the *sensation* derived therefrom through our connection with the body. It is only another form of cold or heat; and what are they? They are vibrations; they are *felt;* they do not really exist in themselves. So we can calmly look on the picture as it passes fragmentarily through those few square feet contained within the superficial boundaries of our elementary frame. We *must* do so, for it is a copy of the greater, of the universal form. For we otherwise will never be able to understand the greater picture. Now, then, is there not many a cubic inch of your own body which is entitled to know and to be the Truth in greater measure than now? And yet you grieve for the ignorance of so many other human beings! Grieve on; and I grieve too. Do not imagine that I *am* what is there written. Not so. I am grieving just the same outwardly, but inwardly trying what I have just told you. And what a dream all this is. Here I am writing you so seriously, and now I see that you know it all quite well and much better than I do.

Yet, my dear Jasper, now and then I feel — not Doubt of Masters who hear any heartbeat in the right direction, but — a terrible Despair of these people. Oh, my God! The age is black as hell, hard as iron. It is iron, it is Kali Yuga. Kali is always painted black. Yet Kali Yuga by its very nature, and terrible, swift momentum, permits one to do more with his energies in a shorter time than in any other Yuga. But heavens, what a combat! Demons from all the spheres; waving clouds of smoky Karma; dreadful shapes; stupefying exhalations from every side. Exposed at each turn to new dangers. Imagine a friend walking with you who you see is in the same road, but all at once he is permeated by these things of death and shows a disposition to obstruct your path, the path of himself. Yes; the gods are asleep for awhile. But noble hearts still walk here, fighting over again the ancient fight. They seek each other, so as to be of mutual help. We will not fail them. To fail would be nothing, but to stop working for Humanity and Brotherhood would be awful. We cannot: we will not. Yet we have not a clear road. No, it is not clear. I am content if I can see the next step in advance only. You seek *The Warrior*. He is here, somewhere. No one can find him for you. You must do that. Still He fights on. No doubt He sees you and tries to make you see Him. Still He fights on and on.

How plainly the lines are drawn, how easily the bands are seen. Some want a certificate, or an uttered pledge, or a secret meeting, or a declaration, but without any of that I see those who — up to this hour — I find are my "companions." They need no such folly. They are there; they hear and understand the battle-cry, they recognize the sign.

Now where are the rest? Many have I halted, and spoken the exact words to them, have exposed to them my real heart, and they heard nothing; they thought that heart was something else. I sigh to think how many. Perhaps I overlooked some; perhaps some did not belong to me. There are some who partly understood the words and the sign, but they are not sure of themselves; they know that they partake of the nature, but are still held back.

Do you not see, Jasper, that your place in the ranks is well known? You need no assurances because they are *within* you. Now what a dreadful letter; but it is all true.

A student of occultism after a while gets into what we may call a psychic whirl, or a vortex of occultism. At first he is affected by the feelings and influences of those about him. That begins to be pushed off and he passes into the whirl caused by the mighty effort of his Higher Self to make him remember his past lives. Then those past lives affect him. They become like clouds throwing shadows on his path. Now they seem tangible and then fade away, only a cloud. Then they begin to affect his impulse to action in many various ways. Today he has vague calling longings to do something, and, critically regarding himself, he cannot see in this life any cause. It is the bugle note of a past life blown almost in his face. It startles him; it may throw him down. Then it starts before him, a phantom, or, like a person behind you as you look at a mirror, it looks over his shoulder. Although dead and past they yet have a power. He gets too a power and a choice. If all his previous past lives were full of good, then irresistible is the force for his benefit. But all alike marshal up in front, and he hastens their coming by his effort. Into this vortex about him others are drawn, and their germs for good or ill ripen with activity. This is a phase of the operation of Karmic stamina. The choice is this. These events arrive one after the other and, as it were, offer themselves. If he chooses wrong, then hard is the fight. The one chosen attracts old ones like itself perhaps, for all have a life of their own. Do you wonder that sometimes in the case of those who rush unprepared into the "circle of ascetics" and before the ripe moment, insanity sometimes results? But then that insanity is their safety for the next life, or for their return to sanity.

Receive my brotherly assurances, my constant desire to help you. Z.

In respect to Karmic action it is well to recall the statement of Patanjali that "works exist only in the shape of mental deposits" (Book 2, Aph. 12, A). By "works" is here meant Karma, the stock of works, or Action. Its results remain as mental deposits or potential energies in the higher part of the fifth principle, and when it reincarnates those seeds are there to "ripen on the tablets of the mind" whenever they are exposed to favoring circumstances. Sometimes they remain dormant for want of something to arouse them, as in the case of children. "The mental deposits of works, collected from time without beginning in the ground of the mind, as they by degrees arrive at maturation, so do they, existing in lesser or greater measure (the sum of merit being less than that of demerit, or conversely) lead to their effects in the shape of rank, raised or lowered, . . . or experience of good or ill" (Book 2, Aph. 13, B). The mind energizes and impels us to fresh action. The impulse lies within, in germ, and may be ripened by interior or exterior suggestion. Can we, then, be too careful to guard the ground of the mind, to keep close watch over our thoughts? These thoughts are dynamic. Each one as it leaves the mind has a *vis viva* of its own, proportionate to the intensity with which it was propelled. As the force or work done, of a moving body, is proportionate to the square of its velocity, so we may say that the force of thoughts is to be measured by the square or quadrupled power of their spirituality, so greatly do these finer forces increase by activity. The spiritual force, being impersonal, fluidic, not bound to any constricting center, acts with unimaginable swiftness. A thought, on its departure from the mind, is said to associate itself with an elemental; it is attracted wherever there is a similar vibration, or, let us say, a suitable soil, just as the winged thistle-seed floats off and sows itself in this spot and not in that, in the soil of its natural selection. Thus the man of virtue, by admitting a material or sensual thought into his mind, even though he expels it, sends it forth to swell the evil impulses of the man of vice from whom he imagines himself separated by a wide gulf, and to whom he may have just given a fresh impulse to sin. Many men are like sponges, porous and bibulous, ready to suck up every element of the order preferred by their nature. We all have more or less of this quality: we attract what we love, and we may derive a greater strength from the vitality of thoughts infused from without than from those self-reproduced within us at a time when our nervous vitality is exhausted. It is a solemn thought, this, of our responsibility for the impulse of another. We live in one another, and our widely different deeds have often a common source. The occultist cannot go far upon his way without realizing to what a great extent he is "his brother's keeper." Our affinities are ourselves, in whatever ground they may live and ripen. J. N.

VIII

DEAR JASPER:

I seize a few moments to acknowledge your letter. This is a period of waiting, of silence. Nothing seems alive. All oracles are silent. But the great clock of the Universe still goes on, unheeding. On Sunday I engaged in Meditation and received some benefit. I wished I could see you to speak of it. Yet these things are too high for words, and when we approach the subjects we are not able to give expression to our thoughts. We do not live up to our highest soul possibilities. All that prevents our reaching up to the high thoughts of the far past is our own weakness, and not the work of any other. How petty seem the cares of this earth when we indulge in deep reflection; they are then seen for what they are, and later on they are obliterated. It is true that the road to the gods is dark and difficult, and, as you say, we get nothing from them at first call: we have to call often. But we can on the way stop to look ahead, for no matter how sombre or howsoever weak ourselves, the Spectator sees it all and beckons to us, and whispers, "Be of good courage, for I have prepared a place for you where you will be with me forever." He is the Great Self; He is ourselves.

The Leaders of the world are always trying to aid us. May we pass the clouds and see them ever. All our obstructions are of our own making. All our power is the storage of the past. That store we all must have; who in this life feels it near is he who has in this life directed his thoughts to the proper channel. That others do not feel it is because they have lived but blindly. That you do not feel it and see it more is because you have not yet directed all your mental energies to it. This great root of Karmic energy can be drawn upon by directing the fire of our minds in that direction. Towards Love of course is the right way; the Love of the Divine and of all beings. If we feel that after all we are not yet "Great Souls" who participate in the totality of those "Souls who wait upon the gods," it need not cast us down: we are waiting our hour in hope. Let us wait patiently, in the silence which follows all effort, knowing that thus Nature works, for in her periods of obscuration she does naught where that obscuration lies, while doubtless she and we too are then at work on other spheres.

That described by you is not the soul; it is only a partial experience. Did you know the Soul, then could you yourself reply to all those questions, for all knowledge is there. In the soul is every creature and every thought alike. That sinking down of your thoughts to the center is practice. It can be done and we cannot explain it; we can only say "do it." Still do not hunger to do these things. The first step in *becoming* is resignation. Resignation is the sure, true, and royal road. Our subtle motives, ever changing, elude us when we seek it. You are near to it; it needs a great care. But while the body may be requiring time to feel its full results, we can instantly change the attitude of the mind. After Resignation, follow (in their own order) Satisfaction, Contentment, Knowledge. Anxiety to do these things is an obscurant and deterrent. So try to acquire patient Resignation. The lesson intended by the Karma of your present life is *the higher patience*. I can tell you nothing on this head; it is a matter for self and practice. Throw away every wish to get the power, and seek only for understanding of thyself. Insist on carelessness. Assert to yourself that it is not of the slightest consequence what you were yesterday, but in every moment strive for that moment; the results will follow of themselves.

The Past! What is it? Nothing. Gone! Dismiss it. You are the past of yourself. Therefore it concerns you not as such. It only concerns you as you now are. In you, as now you exist, lies *all* the past. So follow the Hindu maxim: "Regret nothing; never be sorry; and cut all doubts with the sword of spiritual knowledge." Regret is productive only of error. I care not what I *was*, or what any one *was*. I only look for what I am each moment. For as each moment is and at once is not, it must follow that if we think of the past we forget the present, and while we forget, the moments fly by us, making more past. Then regret nothing, not even the greatest follies of your life, for they are gone, and you are to work in the present which is both past and future at once. So then, with that absolute knowledge that all your limitations are due to Karma, past or in this life, and with a firm reliance ever now upon Karma as the only judge, who will be good or bad as you make it yourself, you can stand anything that may happen and feel serene despite the occasional despondencies which all feel, but which the light of Truth always dispels. This verse always settles everything: —

"In him who knows that all spiritual beings are the same in kind with the Supreme Being, what room can there be for delusion and what room for sorrow when he reflects upon the unity of spirit?"

In all these inner experiences there are tides as well as in the ocean. We rise and fall. Anon the gods descend, and then they return to heaven. Do not *think* of getting them to descend, but strive to raise *yourself* higher on the road down which they periodically return, and thus get nearer to them, so that you shall in fact receive their influences sooner than before.

Adios. May you ever feel the surge of the vast deeps

that lie beyond the heart's small ebb. Perhaps our comrades are coming nearer. Who knows? But even if not, then we will wait; the sun must burst some day from the clouds. This will keep us strong while, in the company of the Dweller of the Threshold, we have perforce to stare and sham awhile.

Z.

The "higher patience" alluded to also requires a care. It is the fine line between pride and humility. Both are extremes and mistakes; oscillations from one to the other are only a trifle better. How shall we be proud when we are so small? How dare we be humble when we are so great? In both we blaspheme. But there is that firm spot between the two which is the place "neither too high nor too low" on which Krishna told Arjuna to sit; a spot *of his own*. It is the firm place which our faith has won from the world. On it we are always to stand calmly, not overshadowed by any man however great, because each of us contains the potentialities of every other. "Not overshadowed" does not mean that we are not to show reverence to those through whom the soul speaks. It is the great soul we reverence, and not the mortal clay. We are to examine thoughtfully all that comes to us from such persons, and all that comes to us from any source wearing the aspect of truth, and try faithfully to see wherein it may be true, laying it aside, if we fail, as fruit not ripe for us yet. We are not to yield up our intuitions to any being, while we may largely doubt our judgment at all times. We are not to act without the inner asseveration, but we must not remain ignorant of the serious difficulty of separating this intuitive voice from the babble and prattle of fancy, desire, or pride. If we are just to ourselves we shall hold the balance evenly. How can we be just to any other who are not just to ourselves? In the Law a man suffers as much from injustice to himself as to another; it matters not in whose interests he has opposed the universal currents; the Law only knows that he has tried to deflect them by an injustice. It takes no account of persons nor even of ignorance of the Law. It is an impartial, impersonal force, only to be understood by the aid of the higher patience, which at once dares all and endures all.

"Never regret anything." Regret is a thought, hence an energy. If we turn its tide upon the past, it plays upon the seeds of that past and vivifies them; it causes them to sprout and grow in the ground of the mind: from thence to expression in action is but a step. A child once said to me when I used the word "Ghosts," "Hush! Don't think of them. What we think of always happens." There are no impartial observers like children when they think away from themselves. J. N.

IX

Dear Sir and Brother:

Tell your friend and inquirer this. No one was ever converted into Theosophy. Each one who *really* comes into it does so because it is only "an extension of previous beliefs." This will show you that Karma is a true thing. For no idea we get is any more than an extension of previous ones. That is, they are cause and effect in endless succession. Each one is the producer of the next and inheres in that successor. Thus we are all different and some similar. My ideas of today and yours are tinged with those of youth, and we will thus forever proceed on the inevitable line we have marked out in the beginning. We of course alter a little always, but never until our old ideas are extended. Those *false* ideas now and then discarded are not to be counted; yet they give a shadow here and there. But through Brotherhood we receive the knowledge of others, which we consider until (if it fits us) it is ours. As far as your private conclusions are concerned, use your discrimination always. Do not adopt any conclusions merely because they are uttered by one in whom you have confidence, but adopt them when they coincide with your intuition. To be even unconsciously deluded by the influence of another is to have a counterfeit faith.

Spiritual knowledge includes every action. Inquirers ought to read the *Bhagavad-Gîtâ*. It will give them food for centuries if they read with spiritual eyes at all. Underneath its shell is the living spirit that will light us all. I read it ten times before I saw things that I did not see at first. In the night the ideas contained in it are digested and returned partly next day to the mind. It is the study of adepts.

Let no man be unaware that while there is a great joy in this belief there is also a great sorrow. Being true, being *the Law*, all the great forces are set in motion by the student. He now thinks he has given up ambition and comfort. The ambition and comfort he has given up are those of the lower plane, the mere reflections of the great ambitions and comforts of a larger life. The rays of truth burn up the covers time has placed upon those seeds, and then the seeds begin to sprout and cause new struggles. Do not leave any earnest inquirer in ignorance of this. It has cost others many years and tears of blood to self-learn it.

How difficult the path of action is! I see the future dimly, and unconsciously in such case one makes efforts either for or against it. Then Karma results. I could almost wish I did not hear these whispers. But he who conquers himself is greater than the conquerors of worlds.

Perhaps you see more clearly now how Karma operates. If one directs himself to eliminating all old Karma, the struggle very often becomes tremendous, for the whole load of ancient sin rushes to the front on a man and the events succeed each other rapidly; the strain is terrific, and the whole life fabric groans and rocks. As is said in the East, you may go through the appointed course in 700 births, in seven years, or in seven minutes.

The sentence in *Light on the Path* referred to by so many students is not so difficult as some others. One answer will do for all. The book is written on the basis of Reincarnation, and when it says the soiled garment will fall again on you, it means that this will happen in some other life, not necessarily in this, though that may be too. To "turn away in horror" is *not* detachment. Before we can hope to prevent any particular state of mind or events reaching us in this or in another life, *we* must in fact be detached from these things. Now *we* are not our bodies or mere minds, but the *real* part of us in which Karma inheres. Karma brings everything about. It attaches to our real inner selves by attachment and repulsion. That is, if we love vice or anything, it seizes on us by attachment thereto; if we hate anything, it seizes on our inner selves by reason of the strong horror we feel for it. In order to prevent a thing we must understand it; we cannot understand while we fear or hate it. We are not to love vice, but are to recognize that it is a part of the whole, and, trying to understand it, we thus get above it. This is the "doctrine of opposites" spoken of in *Bhagavad-Gîtâ*. So if we turn in horror now (we may feel sad and charitable, though) from the bad, the future life will feel that horror and develop it by reaction into a reincarnation in a body and place where we must in material life go through the very thing we hate now. As we are striving to reach God, we must learn to be as near like Him as possible. He loves and hates not; so we must strive to regard the greatest vice as being something we must not hate while we will not engage in it, and then we may approach that state where we will know the greater love that takes in good and evil men and things alike.

Good and Evil are only the two poles of the one thing. In the Absolute, Evil is the same thing in this way. One with absolute knowledge can *see* both good and evil, but he does not *feel* Evil to be a thing to flee from, and thus he has to call it merely the other pole. We say Good or Evil as certain events seem pleasant or unpleasant to us or our present civilization. And so we have coined those two words. They are bad words to use. For in the Absolute one is just as necessary as the other, and often what seem evil and "pain" are not absolutely so, but only necessary adjustments in the progress of the soul. Read *Bhagavad-Gîtâ* as to how the self seems to suffer pain. What is Evil now? Loss of friends? No; if you are self-centered. Slander? Not if you rely on Karma. There is only evil when you rebel against immutable decrees that must be worked out. You know that there must be these balancings which we call Good and Evil. Just imagine one man who really was a high soul, now living as a miser and enjoying it. You call it an evil; he a good. Who is right? You say "Evil" because you are speaking out of the True; but the True did know that he could never have passed some one certain point unless he had that experience, and so we see him now in an evil state. Experience we must have, and if we accept it at our own hands we are wise. That is, while striving to do our whole duty to the world and ourselves, we will not live the past over again by vain and hurtful regrets, nor condemn any man, whatever his deeds, since we cannot know their true cause. We are not Karma, we are not the Law, and it is a species of that hypocrisy so deeply condemned by It for us to condemn any man. That the Law lets a man live is proof that he is not yet judged by that higher power. Still we must and will keep our discriminating power at all times.

As to rising above Good and Evil, that does not mean to do evil, of course. But, in fact, there can be no *real* Evil or Good; if our aim is right our acts cannot be evil. Now all acts are dead when done; it is in the heart that they are conceived and are already there done; the mere bodily carrying out of them is a dead thing in itself. So we may do a supposed good act and that shall outwardly appear good, and yet as our motive perhaps is wrong the act is naught, but the motive counts.

The great God did all, good and bad alike. Among the rest are what appear Evil things, yet he must be unaffected. So if we follow *Bhagavad-Gîtâ*, second chapter, we must do only those acts we believe right for the sake of God and not for ourselves, and if we are regardless of the consequences we are not concerned if they *appear* to be Good or Evil. As the heart and mind are the real planes of error, it follows that we must look to it that we do all acts merely because they are there to be done. It then becomes difficult only to separate ourselves from the act.

We can never as human beings rise above being the instruments through which that which is called Good and Evil comes to pass, but as that Good and Evil are the result of comparison and are not in themselves absolute, it must follow that we (the real *"we"*) must learn to rise internally to a place where these occurrences appear to us merely as changes in a life of change. Even in the worldly man this sometimes happens.

As, say Bismarck, used to moving large bodies of men and perhaps for a good end, can easily rise above the transient Evil, looking to a greater result. Or the physician is able to rise above pain to a patient, and only consider the good, or rather the result, that is to follow from a painful operation. The patient himself does the same.

So the student comes to see that he is not to do either "Good" or "Evil," but to do any certain number of acts set before him, and meanwhile not ever to regard much his line of conduct, but rather his line of motive, for his conduct follows necessarily from his motive. Take the soldier. For him there is nothing better than lawful war. Query. Does he do wrong in warring or not, even if war unlawful? He does not unless he mixes his motive. They who go into war for gain or revenge do wrong, but not he who goes at his superior's orders, because it is his present duty.

Let us, then, extend help to all who come our way. This will be true progress; the veils that come over our souls fall away when we work for others. Let that be the real motive, and the *quality* of work done makes no difference.   Z.

It would seem that Good and Evil are not inherent in things themselves, but in the uses to which those things are put by us. They are conditions of manifestation. Many things commonly called immoral are consequences of the unjust laws of man, of egotistic social institutions: such things are not immoral *per se*, but relatively so. They are only immoral in point of time. There are others whose evil consists in the base use to which higher forces are put, or to which Life — which is sacred — is put, so that here also evil does not inhere in them, but in ourselves; in our misuse of noble instruments in lower work. Nor does evil inhere in us, but in our ignorance; it is one of the great illusions of Nature. All these illusions cause the soul to experience in matter until it has consciously learned every part: then it must learn to know the whole and all at once, which it can only do by and through re-union with Spirit; or with the Supreme, with the Deity.

If we take, with all due reverence, so much of the standpoint of the Supreme as our finite minds or our dawning intuition may permit, we feel that he stands above unmoved by either Good or Evil. Our good is relative, and evil is only the limitation of the soul by matter. From the material essence of the Deity all the myriad differentiations of Nature (Prakriti, cosmic substance), all the worlds and their correlations are evolved. They assist the cyclic experience of the soul as it passes from state to state. How, then, shall we say that any state is evil in an absolute sense? Take murder. It seems an evil. True, we cannot *really* take life, but we can destroy a vehicle of the divine Principle of Life and impede the course of a soul using that vehicle. But we are more injured by the deed than any other. It is the fruit of a certain unhealthy state of the soul. The deed sends us to hell, as it were, for one or more incarnations; to a condition of misery. The shock, the natural retribution, our own resultant Karma, both the penalties imposed by man and that exacted by occult law, chasten and soften the soul. It is passed through a most solemn experience which had become necessary to its growth and which in the end is the cause of its additional purification. In view of this result, was the deed evil? It was a necessary consequence of the limitations of matter; for had the soul remained celestial and in free Being, it could not have committed murder. Nor has the immortal soul, the spectator, any share in the wrong; it is only the personality, the elementary part of the soul, which has sinned. All that keeps the soul confined to material existence is evil, and so we cannot discriminate either. The only ultimate good is Unity, and in reality nothing but that exists. Hence our judgments are in time only. Nor have we the right to exact a life for a life. "Vengeance is mine, saith the Lord (Law); I will repay." We become abetters of murder in making such human laws. I do not say that every experience must be gone through bodily, because some are lived out in the mind. Nor do I seek to justify any. The only justification is in the Law.

The innocent man unjustly murdered is rewarded by Karma in a future life. Indeed, any man murdered is reimbursed, so to say; for while that misfortune sprang from his Karma, occult law does not admit of the taking of life. Some men are the weapons of Karma in their wrong-doing, but they themselves have appointed this place to themselves in their past.

The Great Soul needed just that body, whatever the errors of its nature or its physical environment, and to disappoint the soul is a fearful deed for a man. For it is only man, only the lower nature under the influence of Tamas (the quality of darkness), which feels the impulse to take life, whether in human justice, for revenge, for protection, or so on. "The soul neither kills nor is killed." What we know as ourselves is only the natural man, the lower principles and mind, presided over by the false consciousness. Of the soul we have but brief and partial glimpses — in conscience or intuition — in our ordinary state. There are, of course, psychic and spiritual states in which more is known. Thus nature wars against nature, always for the purpose of bringing about the purification and evolution of the soul. Nature exists only for the purpose of the soul. If we think out the subject upon these lines, we can at least see how rash we should be to conclude that any deed was unmixed evil, or that these distinctions exist in the Absolute. It alone is; all else is phenomenal and transitory; these differences disappear as we proceed upward. Meanwhile we are to avoid all these immoral things and many others not so regarded by the crowd at all, but which are just as much so because we know to what increased ignorance and darkness they give rise through the ferment which they cause in the nature, and that this impedes the entrance of the clear rays of Truth.

I doubt that the soul knows the moral or immoral. For just consider for a moment the case of a disembodied soul. What is sin to it when freed from that shell — the body? What does it know then of human laws or moralities, or the rules and forms of matter? Does it even see them? What lewdness can it commit? So I say that these moralities are of this plane only, to be heeded and obeyed there, but not to be postulated as final or used as a balance to weigh the soul which has other laws. The free soul has to do with essences and powers all impersonal; the strife of matter is left behind. Still higher and above as within all, the passionless, deathless spirit looks down, knowing well that, when the natural has once again subsided into its spiritual source, all this struggle and play of force and will, this waxing and waning of forms, this progression of consciousness, which throw up coming clouds and fumes of illusion before the eye of the soul, will have come to an end. Even now, while we cannot master these high themes, we can have a patient trust in the processes of evolution and the Law, blaming and judging no man, but living up to our highest intuitions ourselves. *The real test of a man is his motive*, which we do not see, nor do his acts always represent it.

J. N.

X

DEAR JASPER:

You ask me about the "three qualities sprung from Nature," mentioned in the *Bhagavad-Gîtâ*. They exist potentially (latent) in *Purush* (Spirit), and during that time spoken of in the *Bhagavad-Gîtâ* as the time when He produces all things after having devoured them (which is the same thing as Saturn devouring his children), they come forth into activity, and therefore are found *implicating* all beings, who are said not to be free from their influence.

"Beings" here must refer to formed beings in all worlds. Therefore in these forms the qualities *exist* [for *form* is derived from Nature = Prakriti = Cosmic Substance. — J. N.], and at the same time *implicate* the spectator (soul) who is in the form. The Devas are gods — that is, a sort of spiritual power who are lower than the Ishwara in man. They are influenced by the quality of Satwa, or Truth. They enjoy a period of immense felicity of enormous duration, but which having *duration* is not an eternity.

It is written: "Goodness, badness, and indifference — the qualities thus called — sprung from Nature, influence the imperishable soul within the body."

This imperishable soul is thus separated from the body in

which the qualities influence it, and also from the qualities which are not it. It is Ishwara. The Ishwara is thus implicated by the qualities.

The first or highest quality is Satwa, which is in its nature pure and pleasant, and implicates Ishwara by connection with pleasant things and with knowledge. Thus even by dwelling in Satwa the soul is implicated.

The second quality is Raja and causes action; it implicates the soul because it partakes of avidity and propensity, and causing actions thus implicates the soul.

The third, Tamo quality, is of the nature of indifference and is the deluder of all mortals. It is fed by ignorance.

Here, then, are two great opposers to the soul, *ignorance* and *action*. For action proceeding from Raja assisted by Satwa does not lead to the highest place; while ignorance causes destruction. Yet when one knows that he is ignorant, he has to perform actions in order to destroy that ignorance. How to do that without always revolving in the whirl of action [Karma, causing rebirths. — J. N.] is the question.

He must first get rid of the idea that he himself really does anything, knowing that the actions all take place in these three natural qualities, and not in the soul at all. The word "qualities" must be considered in a larger sense than that word is generally given.

Then he must place all his actions on devotion. That is, sacrifice all his actions to the Supreme and not to himself. He must either (leaving out indifference) set himself up as the God to whom he sacrifices, or the other real God — Krishna, and all his acts and aspirations are done either for himself or for the All. Here comes in the importance of motive. For if he performs great deeds of valor, or of benefit to man, or acquires knowledge so as to assist man, and is moved to that merely because he thinks *he* will attain salvation, he is only acting for his own benefit and is therefore sacrificing to himself. Therefore he must be devoted inwardly to the All; that is, he places all his actions on the Supreme, knowing that he is not the doer of the actions, but is the mere witness of them.

As he is in a mortal body, he is affected by doubts which will spring up. When they do arise, it is because he is ignorant about something. He should therefore be able to disperse doubt "by the sword of knowledge." For if he has a ready answer to some doubt, he disperses that much. All doubts come from the lower nature, and *never* in any case from higher nature. Therefore as he becomes more and more devoted he is able to know more and more clearly the knowledge residing in his Satwa part. For it says:

"A man who, perfected in devotion (or who persists in its cultivation) finds spiritual knowledge spontaneously in himself in progress of time." Also: "The man of doubtful mind enjoys neither this world nor the other (the Deva world), nor final beatitude."

The last sentence is to destroy the idea that if there is in us this higher self it will, even if we are indolent and doubtful, triumph over the necessity for knowledge, and lead us to final beatitude in common with the whole stream of man.

The three qualities are lower than a state called Turya, which is a high state capable of being enjoyed even while in this body. Therefore in that state, there exists none of the three qualities, but there the soul sees the three qualities moving in the ocean of Being beneath. This experience is not only met with after death, but, as I said, it may be enjoyed in the present life, though of course consciously very seldom. But even consciously there are those high Yogees who can and do rise up to Nirvana, or Spirit, while on the earth. This state is the fourth state, called Turya. There is no word in English which will express it. In that state the body is alive though in deep catalepsy. [Self-induced by the Adept. — J. N.] When the Adept returns from it he brings back *whatever he can* of the vast experiences of that Turya state. Of course they are far beyond any expression, and their possibilities can be only dimly perceived by us. I cannot give any description thereof because I have not known it, but I perceive the possibilities, and you probably can do the same.

It is well to pursue some kind of practice, and pursue it either in a fixed place, or in a mental place which cannot be seen, or at night. The fact that what is called Dharana, Dhyana, and Samâdhi may be performed should be known. (See Patanjali's yoga system.)

Dharana is selecting a thing, a spot, or an idea, to fix the mind on.

Dhyana is contemplation of it.

Samâdhi is meditating on it.

When attempted, they of course are all one act.

Now, then, take what is called the well of the throat or pit of the throat.

1st. Select it. — Dharana.

2d. Hold the mind on it. — Dhyana.

3d. Meditate on it. — Samâdhi.

This gives firmness of mind.

Then select the spot in the head where the Shushumna nerve goes. Never mind the location; call it the top of the head. Then pursue the same course. This will give some insight into spiritual minds. At first it is difficult, but it will grow easy by practice. If done at all, the same hour of each day should be selected, as creating a habit, not only in the body, but also in the mind. Always keep the direction of Krishna in mind: namely, that it is done for the whole body corporate of humanity, and not for one's self.

As regards the passions: Anger seems to be the *force* of Nature; there is more in it, though.

Lust (so called) is the gross symbol of love and desire to create. It is the perversion of the True in love and desire.

Vanity, I think, represents in one aspect the illusion-power of Nature; Maya, that which we mistake for the reality. It is nearest always to us and most insidious, just as Nature's illusion is ever present and difficult to overcome.

Anger and Lust have some of the Rajasika quality; but it seems to me that Vanity is almost wholly of the Tamo-gunam.

May you cross over to the fearless shore.   Z.

As regards the practices of concentration suggested in this letter, they are only stages in a life-long contemplation; they are means to an end, means of a certain order among means of other orders, all necessary, the highest path being that of constant devotion and entire resignation to the Law. The above means have a physiological value because the spots suggested for contemplation are, like others, vital centers. Excitation of these centers, and of the magnetic residue of breath always found in them, strengthens and arouses the faculties of the inner man, the magnetic vehicle of the soul and the link between matter and spirit. This is a form of words necessary for clearness, because in reality matter and spirit are one. We may better imagine an infinite series of force correlations which extend from pure Spirit to its grossest vehicle, and we may say that the magnetic inner vehicle, or astral man, stands at the half-way point of the scale. The secret of the circulation of the nervous fluid is hidden in these vital centers, and he who discovers it can use the body at will. Moreover, this practice trains the mind to remain in its own principle, without energizing, and without exercising its tangential force, which is so hard to overcome. Thought has a self-reproductive power, and when the mind is held steadily to one idea it becomes colored by it, and, as we may say, all the correlates of that thought arise within the mind. Hence the mystic obtains knowledge about any object of which he thinks constantly in fixed contemplation. Here is the rationale of Krishna's words: "Think constantly of me; depend on me alone; and thou shalt surely come unto me."

The pure instincts of children often reveal occult truths. I heard a girl of fifteen say recently: "When I was a small child I was always supposin'. I used to sit on the window seat and stare, stare, at the moon, and I was supposin' that, if I only stared long enough, I'd get there and know all about it."

Spiritual culture is attained through concentration. It must be continued daily and every moment to be of use. The "Elixir of Life" *(Five Years of Theosophy)* gives us some of the reasons for this truth. Meditation has been defined as "the cessation of active, external thought." Concentration is the entire life-tendency to a given end. For example, a devoted mother is one who consults the interests of her children and all branches of their interests in and before all things; not one who sits down to think fixedly about one branch of their interests all the day. Life is the great teacher; it is the great manifestation of Soul, and

Soul manifests the Supreme. Hence all methods are good, and all are but parts of the great aim, which is Devotion. "Devotion is success in actions," says the *Bhagavad-Gîtâ*. We must use higher and lower faculties alike, and beyond those of mind are those of the Spirit, unknown but discoverable. The psychic powers, as they come, must also be used, for they reveal laws. But their value must not be exaggerated, nor must their danger be ignored. They are more subtle intoxicants than the gross physical energies. He who relies upon them is like a man who gives way to pride and triumph because he has reached the first wayside station on the peaks he has set out to climb. Like despondency, like doubt, like fear, like vanity, pride, and self-satisfaction, these powers too are used by Nature as traps to detain us. Every occurrence, every object, every energy may be used for or against the great end: in each Nature strives to contain Spirit, and Spirit strives to be free. Shall the substance paralyze the motion, or shall the motion control the substance? The interrelations of these two is manifestation. The ratio of activity governs spiritual development; when the great Force has gained its full momentum, It carries us to the borders of the Unknown. It is a force intelligent, self-conscious, and spiritual: Its lower forms, or vehicles, or correlates may be evoked by us, but Itself comes only of Its own volition. We can only prepare a vehicle for It, in which, as Behmen says, "the Holy Ghost may ride in Its own chariot."

"The Self cannot be known by the *Vedas*, nor by the understanding, nor by much learning. He whom the Self chooses, by him alone the Self can be gained."

"The Self chooses him as his own. But the man who has not first turned aside from his wickedness, who is not calm and subdued, *or whose mind is not at rest*, he can never obtain the Self, even by knowledge."

The italics are mine; they indicate the value of that stage of contemplation hitherto referred to as that in which the mind has ceased to energize, and when the pure energies of Nature go to swell the fountain of Spirit.

In regard to the phrase in the above letter that the Adept "brings back *what he can*" from Turya, it is to be understood as referring to the fact that all depends upon the co-ordination of the various principles in man. He who has attained perfection or Mahâtmaship has assumed complete control of the body and informs it at will. But, of course, while in the body he is still, to some extent, as a soul of power, limited by that body or vehicle. That is to say, there are experiences not to be shared by that organ of the soul called by us "the body," and beyond a certain point its brain cannot reflect or recall them. The point varies according to the degree of attainment of individual souls, and while in some it may be a high point of great knowledge and power, still it must be considered as limited compared with those spiritual experiences of the freed soul.

The work upon which all disciples are employed is that of rendering the body more porous, more fluidic, more responsive to all spiritual influences which arise in the inner center, in the soul which is an undivided part of the great Soul of all, and less receptive of the outside material influences which are generated by the unthinking world and by those qualities which are in nature. Abstract thought is said to be "the power of thinking of a thing apart from its qualities"; but these qualities are the phenomenal, the evident, and they make the most impression upon our senses. They bewilder us, and they form a part of that trap which

Nature sets for us lest we discover her inmost secret and rule her. More than this: our detention as individual components of a race provides time for that and other races to go through evolutionary experience slowly, provides long and repeated chances for every soul to amend, to return, to round the curve of evolution. In this Nature is most merciful, and even in the darkness of the eighth sphere to which souls of *spiritual* wickedness descend, her impulses provide opportunities of return if a single responsive energy is left in the self-condemned soul.

Many persons insist upon a perfect moral code tempered by social amenities, forgetting that these vary with climate, nationalities, and dates. Virtue is a noble offering to the Lord. But insomuch as it is mere bodily uprightness and mere mental uprightness, it is insufficient and stands apart from uprightness of the psychic nature or the virtue of soul. The virtue of the soul is true Being; its virtue is, to be free. The body and the mind are not sharers in such experiences, though they may afterward reflect them, and this reflection may inform them with light and power of their own kind. Spirituality is not virtue. It is impersonality, in one aspect. It is as possible to be spiritually "wicked" as to be spiritually "good." These attributes are only conferred upon spirituality by reason of its use for or against the great evolutionary Law, which must finally prevail because it is the Law of the Deity, an expression of the nature and Being of the Unknown, which nature is towards manifestation, self-realization, and reabsorption. All that clashes with this Law by striving for separate existence must in the long run fail, and any differentiation which is in itself incapable of reabsorption is reduced to its original elements, in which shape, so to say, it can be reabsorbed.

Spirituality is, then, a condition of Being which is beyond expression in language. Call it a rate of vibration, far beyond our cognizance. Its language is the language of motion, in its incipiency, and its perfection is beyond words and even thought.

"The knowledge of the Supreme Principle is a divine silence, and the quiescence of all the senses." — *(Clavis of Hermes.)*

"Likes and dislikes, good and evil, do not in the least affect the knower of Brahm, who is bodiless and always existing." — *(Crest Jewel of Wisdom.)*

"Of that nature which is beyond intellect many things are asserted according to intellection, but it is contemplated by a cessation of intellectual energy better than with it." — *(Porphyrios.)*

Thought is bounded, and we seek to enter the boundless. The intellect is the first production of Nature which energizes for the experience of the soul, as I said. When we recognize this truth we make use of that natural energy called Thought for comparison, instruction, and the removal of doubt, and so reach a point where we restrain the outward tendencies of Nature, for, when these are resolved into their cause and Nature is wholly conquered and restrained, that cause manifests itself both in and beyond Nature.

"The incorporeal substances in descending are divided and multiplied about individuals with a diminution of power; but when they ascend by their energies beyond bodies, they become united and exist as a whole by and through exuberance of power." — *(Porphyrios.)*

These hints may suffice for such minds as are already upon the way. Others will be closed to them. Language only expresses the experiences of a race, and since ours has not reached the upper levels of Being we have as yet no words for these things. The East has ever been the home of spiritual research; she has given all the great religions to the world. The Sanscrit has thus terms for some of these states and conditions, but even in the East it is well understood that the formless cannot be expressed by form, or the Illimitable by the limits of words or signs. The only way to know these states is to *be* them: we never can *really* know anything which we are not. J. N.

XI

It has been with regret that I hear of your serious illness, Jasper. While life hangs in the balance, as it would seem yours does and for some time will, you will feel much depression.

Now it is not usual to thus calmly talk to a person of his death, but you do not mind, so I talk. I do not agree with you that death is well. Yours is not a case like that of —— who *was* to die and decided to accept life from Great Powers and work on for Humanity amid all the throes and anguish of that body. Why should you not live now as long as you can in the present body, so that in it you may make all the advance possible and by your life do as much good as you can to the Cause and man? For you have not as yet as Jasper Niemand had a chance to entitle you to *extraordinary* help after death in getting back again soon, so that you would die and run the chance of a long Devachan and miss much that you might do for *Them*. Such are my views. Life is better than death, for death again disappoints the Self. Death is *not* the great informer or producer of knowledge. It is only the great curtain on the stage to be rung up next instant. Complete knowledge must be attained in the triune man: body, soul, and spirit. When that is obtained, then he passes on to other spheres, which to us are unknown and are endless. By living as long as one can, one gives the Self that longer chance.

"Atmanam atmana pashya" (Raise the self by the self — *Gîtâ*) does not seem to be effective after the threshold of death is passed. The union of the trinity is only to be accomplished on earth in a body, and *then* release is desirable.

It is not for myself that I speak, Brother, but for thee, because in death I can lose no one. The living have a greater part in the dead than the dead have in the living.

The doubt which you now feel as to success is morbid. Please destroy it. Better a false hope with no doubt, than much knowledge with doubts of your own chances. "He that doubteth is like the waves of the sea, driven by the wind and tossed." Doubt is not to be solely guarded against when applied to Masters (whom I know you doubt not). It is most to be guarded and repelled in relation to oneself. Any idea that one cannot succeed, or had better die than live because an injured body seems to make success unattainable, is *doubt*.

We dare not hope, but we *dare* try to live on and on that we may serve Them as They serve the Law. We are not to try to be chelas or to do any one thing in this incarnation, but only to know and to be just as much as we can, and the possibility is not measured. Reflect, then, that it [is] only a question of being overcome — by what? By something outside. But if you accuse or doubt yourself, you then give the enemy a rest; he has nothing to do, for you do it all yourself for him, and, leaving you to your fate, he seeks other victims. Rise, then, from this despondency and seize the sword of knowledge. With it, and with Love, the universe is conquerable. Not that I see thee too despondent, Jasper, but I fain would give thee my ideas, even did something kill thee against our will next day.

Am glad that although the body is painful, you yourself are all right. We have in various ways to suffer, and I do not doubt it is a great advance if we can in the midst of physical suffering grasp and hold ourselves calm and away from it. Yet also the body must be rested. Rest, and let the anxieties to do lie still and dormant. By that they are not killed, and when the body gets stronger more is known.

You have been in storms enough. A few moments' reflection will show you that we make our own storms. The power of any and all circumstances is a fixed, unvarying quality, but as *we* vary in our reception of these, it appears to us that our difficulties vary in intensity. They do not at all. We are the variants.

If we admit that we are in the stream of evolution, then each circumstance must be to us quite right. And in our failures to perform set acts should be our greatest helps, for we can in no other way learn that calmness which Krishna insists upon. If all our plans succeeded, then no contrasts would appear to us. Also those plans we make may all be made ignorantly and thus wrongly, and kind Nature will not permit us to carry them out. We get no blame for the plan, but we may acquire Karmic demerit by not accepting the impossibility of achieving. Ignorance of the law cannot be pleaded among men, but ignorance of fact may. In occultism, even if you are ignorant of some facts of importance you are not passed over by *The Law*, for It has regard for no man, and pursues Its adjustments without regard to what we know or are ignorant of.

If you are at all cast down, or if any of us is, then by just that much are our thoughts lessened in power. One could be confined in a prison and yet be a worker for the Cause. So I pray you to remove from your mind any distaste for present circumstances. If you can succeed in looking at it all as *just what you in fact desired*, then it will act not only as a strengthener of your good thoughts, but will reflexly act on your body and make it stronger.

All this reminds me of H., of whose failure you now know. And in this be not disappointed. It could hardly be otherwise. Unwisely he made his demands upon the Law before being quite ready. That is, unwisely in certain senses, for in the greater view naught can be unwise. His apparent defeat, at the very beginning of the battle, is for him quite of course. He went where the fire is hottest and made it hotter by his aspirations. All others have and all will suffer the same. For it makes no difference that his is a bodily affection; as all these things proceed from mental disturbances, we can easily see the same cause under a physical ailment as under a mental divagation. Strangely, too, I wrote you of the few who really do stay, and soon after this news came and threw a light — a red one, so to say — upon the information of H.'s retreat. See how thought interlinks with thought on all planes when the True is the aim.

We ourselves are not wholly exempt, inasmuch as we daily and hourly feel the strain. Accept the words of a fellow traveller; these: Keep up the aspiration and the search, but do not maintain the attitude of despair or the slightest repining. Not that you do. I cannot find the right words; but surely you would know all, were it not that some defects hold you back.

The darkness and the desolation are sure to be ours, but it is only illusionary. Is not the Self pure, bright, bodiless, and free — and art thou not that? The daily waking life is but a penance and the trial of the body, so that *it* too may thereby acquire the right condition. In dreams we see the truth and taste the joys of heaven. In waking life it is ours to gradually distil that dew into our normal consciousness.

Then, too, remember that the influences of this present age are powerful for producing these feelings. What despair and agony of doubt exist today in all places. In this time of upturning, the wise man *waits*. He bends himself, like the reed, to the blast, so that it may blow over his head. Rising, as you do, into the plane where these currents are rushing while you try to travel higher still, you feel these inimical influences, although unknown to you. It is an age of iron. A forest of iron trees, black and forbidding, with branches of iron and brilliant leaves of steel. The winds blow through its arches and we hear a dreadful grinding and crashing sound that silences the still small voice of Love. And its inhabitants mistake this for the voice of God; they imitate it and add to its terrors. Faint not, be not self-condemned. We both are that soundless OM; we rest together upon the bosom of Master. You are not tired; it is that body, now weak, and not only weak but shaken by the force of your own powers, physical and psychical. But the wise man learns to assume in the body an attitude of carelessness that is more careful really than any other. Let that be yours. You are judge. Who accepts you, who dares judge but yourself? Let us wait, then, for natural changes, knowing that if the eye is fixed where the light shines, we shall presently know what to do. This hour is not ripe. But unripe fruit gets ripe, and falls or is plucked. The day must surely strike when you will pluck it down. You are no longer troubled by vain fears or compromises. When the great thought comes near enough, you will go. We must all be servants before we can hope to be masters in the least.

I have been re-reading the life of Buddha, and it fills me with a longing desire to give myself for humanity, to devote myself to a fierce, determined effort to plant myself nearer the altar of sacrifice. As I do not always know just what ought to be done, I must stand on what Master says: "Do what you *can*, if you ever expect to see Them." This being true, and another Adept saying, "Follow the Path They and I show, but do not follow *my* path," why, then, all we can do, whether great or small, is to do just what we can, each in his proper place. It is sure that if we have an immense devotion and do our best, the result will be right for Them and us, even though we would have done otherwise had we known more when we were standing on a course of action. A devoted Chela once said: "I do not mind all these efforts at explanation and all this trouble, for I always have found that that which was done in Master's name was right and came out right." What is done in those names is done without thought of self, and motive is the essential test.

So I am sad and not sad. Not sad when I reflect on the great Ishwar, the Lord, permitting all these antics and shows before our eyes. Sad when I see our weakness and disabilities. We must be serene and do what we can. Ramaswamier rushed off into Sikkhim to try and find Master, and met someone who told him to go back *and do his duty*. That is all any of us can do; often we do not know our duty, but that too is our own fault; it is a Karmic disability.

You ask me how you shall advise your fellow student. The best advice is found in your own letter to me in which you say that the true monitor is within. That is so. Ten thousand Adepts can do one no great good unless we ourselves are ready, and They only act as suggestors to us of what possibilities there are in every human heart. If we dwell within ourselves, and must live and die by ourselves, it must follow that running here and there to see any thing or person does not in itself give progress. Mind, I do not oppose consorting with those who read holy books and are engaged in dwelling on high themes. I am only trying to illustrate my idea that this should not be dwelt on as an end; it is only a means and one of many. There is no help like association with those who think as we do, or like the reading of good books. The best advice I ever saw was to read holy books or whatever books tend to elevate yourself, as you have found by experience. There must be some. Once I found some abstruse theological writings of Plotinus to have that effect on me — very ennobling, and also an explanation of the wanderings of Ulysses. Then there is the *Gîtâ*. All these *are instinct with a life of their own* which changes the vibrations. Vibration is the key to it all. The different states are only differences of vibration, and we do not recognize the astral or other planes because we are out of tune with their vibrations. This is why we now and then dimly feel that others are peering at us, or as if a host of people rushed by us with great things on hand, not seeing us and we not seeing them. It was an instant of synchronous vibration. But the important thing is to develop the Self in the self, and then the possessions of wisdom belonging to all wise men at once belong to us.

Each one would see the Self differently and would yet never see it, for to see it is to *be* it. But for making words we say, "See it." It might be a flash, a blazing wheel, or what not. Then there is the lower self, great in its way, and which must first be known. When first we see it, it is like looking into a glove, and for how many incarnations may it not be so? We look inside the glove and there is darkness; then we have to *go inside* and see that, and so on and on.

The mystery of the ages is man; each one of us. Patience is needed in order that the passage of time required for the bodily instrument to be altered or controlled is complete. Violent control is not as good as gentle control continuous and firmly unrelaxed. The Seeress of Prevorst found that a gentle current did her more good than a violent one would. Gentleness is better because an opposition current is always provoked, and of course if that which produces it is gentle, it will also be the same. This gives the unaccustomed student more time and gradual strength.

I think your fellow-student will be a good instrument, but we must not break the silence of the future lest we raise up unknown and difficult tribes who will not be easy to deal with.

Every situation ought to be used as a means. This is better than philosophy, for it enables us to know philosophy. You do not progress by studying other people's philosophies, for then you do but get their crude ideas. Do not crowd yourself, nor ache to puzzle your brains with another's notions. You have the key to self and that is all; take it and drag out the lurker inside. You are great in generosity and love, strong in faith, and straight in perception. Generosity and love are the abandonment of self. That is your staff. Increase your confidence, not in your abilities, but in the great All being thyself.

I would to God you and all the rest might find peace.

Z.

XII

DEAR JASPER:

There are so many questioners who ask about Chelaship* that your letter comes quite apropos to experiences of my own. You say that these applicants must have some answer, and in that I agree with you. And whether they are ready or unready, we must be able to tell them something. But generally they are not ready, nor, indeed, are they willing to take the first simple step which is demanded. I will talk the matter over with you for your future guidance in replying to such questions; perhaps also to clear up my own mind.

The first question a man should ask himself (and by "man" we mean postulants of either sex) is: "When and how did I get a desire to know about chelaship and to become a chela?"; and secondly, "What is a chela, and what chelaship?"

There are many sorts of chelas. There are lay chelas and probationary ones; accepted chelas and those who are trying to fit themselves to be even lay chelas. Any person can constitute himself a lay chela, feeling sure that he may never in this life consciously hear from his guide. Then as to probationary chelas, there is an *invariable* rule that they go upon seven years' trial. These "trials" do not refer to fixed and stated tests, but to all the events of life and the bearing of the probationer in them. There is no *place* to which applicants can be referred where their request could be made, because these matters do not relate to places and to officials: this is an affair of the inner nature. We *become* chelas; we

---
*Chela means disciple. It is a Sanscrit word. — J. N.

obtain that position in reality because our inner nature is to that extent opened that it can and will take knowledge: we receive the guerdon at the hands of the Law.

In a certain sense every sincere member of the Theosophical Society is in the way of becoming a chela, because the Masters do some of Their work with and for humanity through this Society, selected by Them as Their agent. And as *all* Their work and aspiration are to the end of helping the race, no one of Their chelas can hope to remain (or become) such, if any selfish desire for personal possessions of spiritual wealth constitutes the motive for trying to be a chela. Such a motive, in the case of one already a chela, acts instantly to throw him out of the ranks, whether he be aware of his loss or not, and in the case of one trying to become a chela it acts as *a bar*. Nor does a real chela spread the fact that he is such. For this Lodge is not like exoteric societies which depend upon favor or mere outward appearances. It is a real thing with living Spirit-men at its head, governed by laws that contain within themselves their own executioners, and that do not require a tribunal, nor accusations, nor verdicts, nor any notice whatever.

As a general thing a person of European or American birth has extreme difficulty to contend with. He has no heredity of psychical development to call upon; no known assembly of Masters or Their chelas within reach. His racial difficulties prevent him from easily seeing within himself; he is not introspective by nature. But even he can do much if he purifies his motive, and either naturally possesses or cultivates an ardent and unshakeable faith and devotion. A faith that keeps him a firm believer in the existence of Masters even through years of non-intercourse. They are generous and honest debtors and always repay. How They repay, and when, is not for us to ask. Men may say that this requires as blind devotion as was ever asked by any Church. *It does,* but it is a blind devotion to Masters who are Truth itself; to Humanity and to yourself, to your own intuitions and ideals. This devotion to an ideal is also founded upon another thing, and that is that a man is hardly ready to be a chela unless he is able to stand *alone* and uninfluenced by other men or events, *for he must stand alone*, and he might as well know this at the beginning as at the end.

There are also certain qualifications which he must possess. These are to be found in *Man: Fragments of Forgotten History* towards the close of the book, so we will not dwell upon them here.

The question of the general fitness of applicants being disposed of, we come to the still more serious point of the relations of Guru and Chela, or Master and Disciple. We want to know what it really is to be a pupil of such a Teacher.

The relation of Guru and Chela is nothing if it is not a spiritual one. Whatever is merely outward, or formal, as the relation established by mere asking and acceptance, is not spiritual, but formal, and is that which arises between *teacher* and *pupil*. Yet even this latter is not in any way despicable, because the teacher stands to his pupil, in so far forth as the relation permits, in the same way as the Guru to his Chela. It is a difference of degree; but this difference of degree is what constitutes the distinction between the spiritual and the material, for, passing along the different shadings from the grossest materiality to as far as we can go, we find at last that matter merges into spirit. (We are now speaking, of course, about what is commonly called *matter*, while we well know that in truth the thing thus designated is not really matter, but an enormous illusion which in itself has no existence. The real matter, called *mulaprakriti* by the Hindus, is an invisible thing or substance of which our matter is a representation. The real matter is what the Hermetists called *primordial earth;* a, for us, intangible phase of matter. We can easily come to believe that what is usually called *matter* is not really such, inasmuch as we find clairvoyants and nervous people seeing through thick walls and closed doors. Were this *matter*, then they could not see through it. But when an ordinary clairvoyant comes face to face with *primordial matter*, he or she cannot see beyond, but is met by a dead wall more dense than any wall ever built by human hands.)

So from earliest times, among all but the modern western people, the teacher was given great reverence by the pupil, and the latter was taught from youth to look upon his preceptor as only second to his father and mother in dignity. It was among these people a great sin, a thing that did one actual harm in his moral being, to be disrespectful to his teacher even in thought. The reason for this lay then, and no less to-day does also lie, in the fact that a long chain of influence extends from the highest spiritual guide who may belong to any man, down through vast numbers of spiritual chiefs, ending at last even in the mere teacher of our youth. Or, to restate it in modern reversion of thought, a chain extends up from our teacher or preceptors to the highest spiritual chief in whose ray or descending line one may happen to be. And it makes no difference whatever, in this occult relation, that neither pupil nor final guide may be aware, or admit, that this is the case.

Thus it happens that the child who holds his teacher in

reverence and diligently applies himself accordingly with faith, does no violence to this intangible but mighty chain, and is benefited accordingly, whether he knows it or not. Nor again does it matter that a child has a teacher who evidently gives him a bad system. This is his Karma, and by his reverent and diligent attitude he works it out, and transcends erstwhile that teacher.

This chain of influence is called the *Guruparampara chain.*

The Guru is the *guide or readjuster*, and may not always combine the function of teacher with it. Z.

XIII

DEAR JASPER:

We now have passed from the mere usual and worldly relations of teacher and pupil to that which we will call the *Lodge* for the nonce.

This Lodge is not to be taken up in the pincers of criticism and analyzed or fixed. It is at once everywhere and nowhere. It contains within its boundaries all real Masters, students, guides, and Gurus, of whatever race or creed or no creed. Of it has been said:

"Beyond the Hall of Learning is the Lodge. It is the whole body of Sages in all the world. It cannot be described even by those who are in it, but the student is not prohibited from imagining what it is like."

So therefore at any time any one of its real teachers or disciples will gladly help any other teacher or disciple. But we are not to conclude that, because all are trying to spread truth and to teach the world, we, who call ourselves chela-aspirants or known chelas of any certain person whom we call Guru, can place ourselves at the same moment under the *direct* tutelage of more than one Guru.

Each man who determines in himself that he will enter the Path, has a Guru. But the time between that determination and the hour when he will really know The Master may be long indeed; in some cases it is very short.

We must now occupy a moment in some consideration of divisions.

Just as the merest private in the army has a general who guides the whole but whom he cannot reach except through the others who are officers, so in this order we find divisions of Gurus as well as divisions of disciples.

There is the Great Guru, who is such to many who never know Him or see Him. Then there are others who know Him, and who are Gurus to a number of chelas, and so on until we may imagine a chela who may be a known Guru to another chela below him.

Then, again, there may be chelas who are acting as Guru — unacknowledged, because *pro tempore* in function — to one or more other chelas.

Now he who makes the resolution above-mentioned, does thereby make a bond that rests in the highest Law. It is not a thing to be lightly done, because its consequences are of a serious nature. Not serious in the way of disasters or awful torments or such, but serious in respect to the clearness and brilliancy of those rays of Truth which we wish to reach us.

We have thereby in a sense — its degree determined by the sincerity and power of our motive — taken ourselves out of the common, vast, moving herd of men who are living — as to this — like dumb animals, and have knocked at a door. If we have reverenced our teacher we will now revere our unknown Guru. We must stand interiorly in a faithful attitude. We must have an abiding, settled faith that nothing may shake. For it is to mighty Karma we have appealed, and as the Guru *is Karma* in the sense that He never acts against Karma, we must not lose faith for an instant. For it is this faith that clears up the air there, and that enables us to get help from all quarters.

Then perhaps this determinant or postulant or neophyte decides for himself that he will for the time take as teacher or guide some other chela whose teachings commend themselves. It is not necessary that any out-spoken words should pass between these two.

But having done this, even in thought, he should then apply himself diligently *to the doctrine of that teacher*, not changing until he really finds he has another teacher or has gone to another class. For if he takes up one merely to dispute and disagree — whether outwardly or mentally, he is thereby in danger of totally obscuring his own mind.

If he finds himself not clearly understanding, then he should with faith try to understand, for if he by love and faith vibrates into the higher meaning of his teacher, his mind is thereby raised, and thus greater progress is gained.

We now come to the possible case of an aspirant of that royal and kingly faith who in some way has really found a person who has advanced far upon *the Path*. To this person he has applied and said: "May I be accepted, and may I be a chela of either thee or some other?"

That person applied to then perhaps says: "Not to me; but I refer you to some other of the same class as yourself, and give you to him to be his chela: serve him." With this the aspirant goes, say to the one designated, and deliberately both agree to it.

Here is a case where the real Master has recommended the aspirant to a co-worker who perchance is some grade higher than our neophyte, and the latter is now in a different position from the many others who are silently striving and working, and learning from any and all teachers, but having no specialized Guru for themselves. This neophyte and his "little guru" are connected by a clear and sacred bond, or else both are mere lying children, playing and unworthy of attention. If the "little guru" is true to his trust, he occupies his mind and heart with it, and is to consider that the chela represents Humanity to him for the time.

We postulated that this "little guru" was in advance of the chela. It must then happen that he says that which is sometimes not clear to his chela. This will all the more be so if his chela is new to the matter. But the chela has deliberately taken that guru, and must try to understand *the doctrine of that teacher.*

The proper function of the Guru is to readjust, and not to pour in vast masses of knowledge expressed in clear and easily comprehended terms. The latter would be a piece of nonsense, however agreeable, and not any whit above what any well-written book would do for its reader.

The faith and love which exist between them act as a stimulus to both, and as a purifier to the mind of the chela.

But if the chela, after a while, meets another person who seems to know as much as his "little guru," and to express it in very easy terms, and the chela determines to take him as a teacher, he commits an error. He may listen to his teaching and admire and profit by it, but the moment he mentally determines and then in words asks the other to be his teacher, he begins to rupture the bond that was just established, and possibly may lose altogether the benefit of both. Not necessarily, however; but certainly, if he acquaints not his "little guru" with the fact of the new adoption of teacher, there will be much confusion in that realm of being wherein both do their real "work"; and when he does acquaint his "little guru" with the fact of the newly-acquired teacher, that older guru will retire.

None of this is meant for those minds which do not regard these matters as sacred. A Guru is a sacred being in that sense. Not, of course, in a general sense — yet even if so regarded *when worthy* it is better for the chela — but in all that pertains to the spiritual and real life. To the high-strung soul this is a matter of *adoption;* a most sacred and valuable thing, not lightly taken up or lightly dropped. For the Guru becomes for the time the spiritual *Father* of the chela; that one who is destined to bring him into life or to pass him on to Him who will do so.

So as the Guru is the *adjuster* in reality, the chela does not — except where the Guru is known to be a great Sage or where the chela does it by nature — give slavish attention to every word. He hears the word and endeavors to assimilate the meaning underneath; and if he cannot understand he lays it aside for a better time, while he presently endeavors to understand what he can. And if even — as is often so in India — he cannot understand at all, he is satisfied to be near the Guru and do what may properly be done for him; for even then his abiding faith will eventually clear his mind, of which there are many examples, and regarding which how appropriate is the line

"They also serve who only stand and wait." Z.

XIV

Dear Jasper:

What I wrote in my last is what may be properly said to earnest inquirers who show by their perseverance that they are not mere idle curiosity-seekers, desirous of beguiling the tedium of life with new experiments and sensations. It is not *what* is done, but the spirit in which the least thing is done for Them who are all, that is counted.

You ask the names of the seven rays or lodges. The names could not be given if known to me. In these matters names are always realities, and consequently to give the name would be to reveal the thing itself. Besides, if the names were given, the ordinary person hearing them would not understand them. Just as if I should say that the name of the first is X, which expresses nothing at all to the mind of the hearing person. All that can be said is that there exist those seven rays, districts, or divisions, just as we say that in a town there are legislators, merchants, teachers, and servants. The difference is that in this case we know all about the town, and know just what those names mean. The name only directs the mind to the idea or essential quality.

Again I must go. But Brothers are never parted while they live for the True alone.   Z.

The foregoing letters point clearly to one conclusion concerning that great Theosophist, Madame Blavatsky, though she is unnamed and perhaps unthought of there. Since she sacrificed — not so calling it herself — all that mankind holds dear to bring the glad tidings of Theosophy to the West, that West, and especially the Theosophical Society, thereby stands to her as a chela to his Guru, in so far as it accepts

Theosophy. Her relation to these Theosophists has its being in the highest Law, and cannot be expunged or ignored. So those who regard her personality, and, finding it discordant from theirs, try to reach The Masters by other means *while disregarding or underrating scornfully her high services*, violate a rule which, because it is not made of man, cannot be broken with impunity. Gratitude and the common sentiment of man for man should have taught them this, without occult teaching at all. Such persons have not reached that stage of evolution where they can learn the higher truths. She who accepts the pains of the rack in the torments of a body sapped of its life force by superb torrents of energy lavished on her high Cause; she who has braved the laughter and anger of two continents, and all the hosts of darkness seen and unseen; she who now lives on, only that she may take to herself the Karma of the Society and so ensure its well being, has no need of any man's praise; but even she has need of justice, because, without that impulse in our hearts and souls toward her, she knows that we must fail for this incarnation. As the babe to the mother, as harvest to the earth, so are all those bound to her who enjoy the fruit of her life. May we try, then, to understand these occult connections brought about by the workings of Karma, and bring them to bear upon our diurnal, as well as our theosophical, life. Madame Blavatsky is for us the next higher link in that great chain, of which no link can be passed over or missed.

In further illustration of this letter, I might cite the case of a friend of mine who was at once fired with Theosophy on first hearing of it and ardently desired to become a chela. Certainly he had known these truths in other lives, for all seemed familiar to him, and, though he was what is called "a man of the world," he accepted the philosophy, measured some of its possibilities intuitively, and while careful to do his duty and cause no jars, he ranged his life, especially his inner life, to suit these views. The question of chelaship assumed great prominence in his mind. He knew of no chelas; knew not where to knock or whom to ask. Reflection convinced him that real chelaship consisted in the inner attitude of the postulant; he remembered magnetic and energic laws, and he said to himself that he could at will constitute himself a chela to the Law, at least so far as his own attitude went, and if this did not satisfy him, it was a proof that he desired some personal reward, satisfaction, or powers in the matter, and that his motive was not pure. He was slow to formulate his desires, even to his own mind, for he would not lightly make demands upon the Law; but he at last determined to put his own motives to the test; to try himself and see if he could stand in the attitude of a faithful chela, unrecognized and apparently unheard. He then recorded in his own mind an obligation to serve Truth and the Law as a chela should, always seeking for light and for further aid if possible, recognizing meanwhile that the obligation was on his side only, and that he had no claims on Masters, and only such as he himself could by the strength of his own purpose institute upon the Law. Wherever he could hear of chelas and their duties he listened or read; he tried to imagine himself in the position of an accepted chela, and to fill, so far as in him lay, the duties of that place, living up to all the light he had. For he held that a disciple should always think and act towards the highest possibilities, whether or not he had yet attained these, and not merely confine himself to that course of action which might be considered suited to his lower class or spiritual estate. He believed that the heart is the creator of all real ties, and it alone. To raise himself by himself was then his task. This attitude he resolved to maintain life after life, if needs were, until at last his birthright should be assured, his claim recognized by the Law.

He met with trials, with coldness from those who felt rather than saw his changed attitude; he met with all the nameless shocks that others meet when they turn against the whirlpool of existence and try to find their way back into the true currents of life. Great sorrows and loneliness were not slow to challenge his indomitable will. But he found work to do; and in this he was most fortunate, for to work for others is the disciple's joy, his share in the Divine life, his first accolade by which he may know that his service is accepted. This man had called upon the Law in faith supreme, and he was answered. Karma sent him a friend, and soon he began to get new knowledge, and after a time information reached him of a place or person where he might apply to become a chela on probation. It was not given him as information usually is; nothing of the sort was told him; but with his extending knowledge and opening faculties a conviction dawned upon him that he might pursue such and such a course. He did so, and his prayer was heard. He said to me afterwards that he never knew whether he would not have shown greater strength of mind by relying wholly upon the reality of his unseen, unacknowledged claim, until the moment should come when Masters should accept and call him. For of course he held the ideal of Masters clearly before his mind all this while. Perhaps his application showed him to be weaker than he supposed, in so far as it might evidence a need on his part for tangible proof of a fact in which his higher nature prompted him to believe without such proof. Perhaps it was but natural and right, on the other hand, that after silent service for some time he should put himself on record at the first opportunity granted him by Karma.

He applied, then. I am permitted to give a portion of the answer he received, and which made clear to him the fact that he was already accepted in some measure before his application, as his intuition had told him. The answer may be of untold value to others, both as clearly setting forth the dangers of forcing one's way ahead of one's race, and also by its advice, admonitions, and evidence that the Great Beings of the Orient deal most frankly and gently with applicants. Also it may mark out a course for those who take the wise plan of testing themselves in silence before pushing their demands upon the Law. For this at once heightens their magnetic vibrations, their evolutionary ratio; their flame burns more brilliantly and attracts all kinds of shapes and influences within its radius, so that the fire is hot about him. And not for him alone: other lives coming in contact with his feel this fierce energy; they develop more rapidly, and, if they have a false or weak place in their nature, it is soon discovered and overthrows them for a time. This is the danger of coming into "the circle of ascetics"; a man must be strong indeed who thus thrusts himself in; it is better as a rule to place oneself in the attitude of a disciple and impose the tests oneself: less opposition is provoked. For forces that are foiled by the Adept may hurl themselves on the neophyte who cannot be protected unless his Karma permits it, and there are always those opposing forces of darkness waiting to thin the ranks of the servitors of the Good Law.

Up to this point, then, we may follow this student, and then we lose sight of him; not knowing whether he progressed or failed, or still serves and waits, because such things are not made known. To tell so much as this is rare, and, since it is permitted, it must be because there are many earnest students in this country who need some such support and information. To these I can say that, if they constitute themselves faithful, unselfish disciples, they are such in the knowledge of the Great Law, so long as they are true, in inmost thought and smallest deed, to the pledges of their heart.

ANSWER TO Y. Says Master:

"*Is Y. fully prepared for the uphill work? The way to the goal he strives to reach is full of thorns and leads through miry quagmires. Many are the sufferings the chela has to encounter; still more numerous the dangers to face and conquer.*

"*May he think over it and choose only after due reflection. No Master appealed to by a sincere soul who thirsts for light and knowledge, has ever turned his face away from the supplicant. But it is the duty of those who call for laborers and need them for their fields, to point out to those who offer themselves in truth and trust for the arduous work, the pitfalls in the soil as the hardship of the task.*

"*If undaunted by this warning Y. persists in his determination, he may regard himself as accepted as* ———. *Let him place himself in such case under the guidance of an older chela. By helping him sincerely and devotedly to carry on his heavy burden, he shall prepare the way for being helped in his turn.*"

(Here follow private instructions.)

"*Verily if the candidate relies upon the Law, if he has patience, trust, and intuition, he will not have to wait too long. Through the great shadow of bitterness and sorrow that the opposing powers delight in throwing over the pilgrim on his way to the Gates of Light, the candidate perceives that shining Light very soon in his own soul, and he has but to follow it. Let him beware, however, lest he mistake the occasional will-o'-the-wisp of the psychic senses for the reflex of the great spiritual Light; that Light which dieth not, yet never lives, nor can it shine elsewhere than on the pure mirror of Spirit. . . .*

"*But Y. has to use his own intuitions. One has to dissipate and conquer the inner darkness before attempting to see into the darkness without; to know one's self before knowing things extraneous to one's senses.*"

And now, may the Powers to which my friend Y. has appealed *be permitted by still greater and much higher Powers* to help him. This is the sincere and earnest wish of his truly and fraternally, △

This letter also shows incidentally how one Adept may serve another still higher by reporting or conveying his reply.

TO ASPIRANTS FOR CHELASHIP

Sincere interest in Theosophic truth is often followed by sincere aspiration after Theosophic life, and the question continually recurs, What are the conditions and the steps to chelaship; to whom should application be made; how is the aspirant to know that it has been granted?

As to the conditions and the discipline of chelaship, not a little has been disclosed in *The Theosophist, Man, Esoteric Buddhism,* and other works upon Theosophy; and some of the qualifications, difficulties, and dangers have been very explicitly set forth by Madame Blavatsky in her article upon "Theosophical Mahatmas" in the *Path* of December, 1886. To everyone cherishing even a vague desire for closer relations to the system of development through which Masters are produced, the thoughtful study of this article is earnestly commended. It will clear the ground of several misconceptions, deepen the sense of the seriousness of such an effort, and excite a healthy self-distrust which is better before than after the gate has been passed.

It is entirely possible, however, that the searching of desire and strength incited by that article may only convince more strongly of sincerity, and that not a few readers may emerge from it with a richer purpose and a deeper resolve. Even where there is not a distinct intention to reach chelaship, there may be an eager yearning for greater nearness to the Masters, for some definite assurance of guidance and of help. In either of these cases the question at once arises before the aspirant, Who is to receive the application, and how is its acceptance to be signified?

The very natural, indeed the instinctive, step of such an aspirant is to write to an officer of the Theosophical Society. None the less is this a mistake. For the Theosophical Society is an *exoteric* body, the Lodge of Masters wholly *esoteric*. The former is a voluntary group of inquirers and philanthropists, with avowed aims, a printed Constitution, and published officers, and, moreover, expressly disavowing any power, as a Society, to communicate with Masters; the latter is an Occult Lodge, of whose address, members, processes, functions, nothing is known. It follows, therefore, that there is no person, no place, no address, to which an aspirant may appeal.

Let it be supposed, however, that such an inquiry is preferred to a person advanced in Occult study, versed in its methods and tests and qualifications. Assuredly his reply would be directly to this effect: —

"If you were now fitted to be an accepted chela, you would of yourself know how, where, and to whom to apply. For the becoming a chela *in reality* consists in the evolution or development of certain spiritual principles latent in every man, and in great measure unknown to your present consciousness. Until these principles are to some degree consciously evolved by you, you are not in practical possession of the means of acquiring the first rudiments of that knowledge which now seems to you so desirable. Whether it is desired by your mind or by your heart is still another important question, not to be solved by any one who has not yet the clue to Self.

"It is true that these qualities can be developed (or forced) by the aid of an Adept. And most applicants for chelaship are actuated by a desire to receive instructions directly from the Masters. They do not ask themselves what they have done to merit a privilege so rare. Nor do they consider that, all Adepts being servants of the Law of Karma, it must follow that, did the applicant now merit their visible aid, he would already possess it and could not be in search of it. The indications of the fulfilment of the Law are, in fact, the partial unfolding of those faculties above referred to.

"You must, then, reach a point other than that where you now stand, before you can even ask to be taken as a chela on probation. All candidates enter the unseen Lodge in this manner, and it is governed by Laws containing within themselves their own fulfilment and not requiring any officers whatever. Nor must you imagine that such a probationer is one who works under constant and known direction of either an Adept or another chela. On the contrary, he is tried and tested for at least seven years, and perhaps many more, before the point is reached when he is either accepted (and prepared for the first of a series of initiations often covering several incarnations), or rejected. And this rejection is not by any body of men just as they incline, but is the natural rejection by Nature. The probationer may or may not hear from his Teacher during this preliminary period; more often he does not hear. He may be finally rejected and not know it, just as some men have been on probation and have not known it until they suddenly found themselves accepted. Such men are those self-developed persons who have reached that point in the natural order after many incarnations, where their expanded faculties have entitled them to an entrance into the Hall of Learning or the spiritual Lodge beyond. And all I say of men applies equally to women.

"When anyone is regularly accepted as a chela on probation, the first and only order he receives (for the present) is to work unselfishly for humanity — sometimes aiding and aided by some older chela — *while striving to get rid of the strength of the personal idea.* The ways of doing this are left to his own intuition entirely, inasmuch as the object is to develop that *intuition* and to bring him to *self-knowledge.* It is his having these powers in some degree that leads to his acceptance as a probationer, so that it is more than probable that you have them not yet save as latent possibilities. In order to have in his turn any title to help, he must work for others, but that must not be his motive for working. He who does not feel irresistibly impelled to serve the Race, whether he himself fails or not, is bound fast by his own personality and cannot progress until he has learned that *the race is himself* and not that body which he now occupies. The ground of this necessity for a pure motive was recently stated in *Lucifer* to be that 'unless the intention is entirely unalloyed, the spiritual will transform itself into the psychic, act on the astral plane, and dire results may be produced by it. The powers and forces of animal nature can be equally used by the selfish and revengeful as by the unselfish and all-forgiving; the powers and forces of spirit lend themselves only to the perfectly pure in heart.'

"It may be stated, however, that even those natural forces cannot be discovered by any man who has not obtained the power of getting rid of his personality in some degree. That an emotional desire to help others does not imply this freedom from personality may be seen by the fact that, if you were now perfected in unselfishness in the *real* sense, you would have a conscious existence separate from that of the body and would be able to quit the body at will: in other words, to be free from all sense of self is to be an Adept, for the limitations of self inhibit progress.

"Hear also the words of the Master, taken from Sinnett's *The Occult World*. 'Perhaps you will better appreciate our meaning when told that in our view the highest aspirations for the welfare of humanity become tainted with selfishness if, in the mind of the philanthropist, there lurks the shadow of a desire for self-benefit or a tendency to do injustice, even when these exist unconsciously to himself.'

"While setting forth these facts, as well as the dangers and difficulties — both those set ones appointed by the laws of the Lodge and the more innumerable ones adjudged by Karma and hastened by the efforts of the neophyte, it should also be stated that the Masters desire to deter no man from entering the path. They are well aware, however, from the repeated trials and records of centuries, and from their knowledge of our racial difficulties, how few are the persons who have any clue to their own real nature, which is the foe they attempt to conquer the moment they become pupils of the occult. Hence They endeavor, so far as Karma permits, to hold unfit individuals back from rash ventures, the results of which would recoil upon their unbalanced lives and drive them to despair. The powers of evil, inadequately defied by the ignorant man, revenge themselves upon him as well as upon his friends, and not upon those who are above their reach. Although these powers are not hideous objective shapes coming in tangible ways, they are none the less real and dangerous. Their descent in such instances cannot be prevented; *it is Karma*.

"To lose all sense of self, then, implies the loss of all that ordinary men most value in themselves. It therefore behooves you to seriously consider these points:

"1st. What is your motive in desiring to be a chela? You think that motive is well known to you, whereas it is hidden deep within you, and by that hidden motive you will be judged. It has flared up from unseen regions upon men sure of themselves, has belched out in some lurid thought or deed of which they esteemed themselves incapable, and has overthrown their life or reason. Therefore test yourself ere Karma tests you.

"2d. What the place and duties of a true neophyte are.

"When you have seriously considered both for twenty-one days, you may, if your desire remains firm, take a certain course open to you. It is this.

"Although you do not now know where you can offer yourself to Masters themselves as a chela on probation, yet, in forming that desire in your heart and in re-affirming it (if you do) after due consideration of these points, you have then to some extent called upon the Law, and it is within your power to constitute yourself a disciple, so far as in you lies, through the purity of your motive and effort *if both are sufficiently sustained*. No one can fix a period when this effort will bear fruit, and, if your patience and faith are not strong enough to bear you through an *unlimited* (so far as you know) period of unselfish work for humanity, you had better resign your present fancy, for it is then no more than that. But if otherwise, you are to work for the spiritual enlightenment of Humanity in and through the Theosophical Society (which much needs such laborers), and in all other modes and planes as you best can, remembering the word of Masters: 'He who does what he can and all that he can, and all that he knows how to do, does enough for us.' This task includes that of divesting yourself of all personality through interior effort, because that work, if done in the right spirit, is even more important to the race than any outward work we can do. Living as you now are, on the outward plane chiefly, your work is due there and is to be done there until your growth shall fit you to pass away from it altogether.

"In following this course you work towards a fixed point under observation — as is, indeed, the whole Theosophic body, which is now, *as a body*, a chela of Masters, but specialized from other members in the sense that your definite aim and trust are understood and taken into consideration by the unseen Founders and the Law. The Theosophical Society then stands to you, for the time being, as any older chela might who was appointed for you to aid and to work under. *You are not*, understand, a chela on probation, since no one without authority can confer or announce such a privilege. But if you succeed in lifting yourself and others spiritually, it will be known, *no matter what the external silence may seem to be*, and you will receive your full dues from Those who are honest debtors and ministers of the Just and Perfect Law. You must be ready to work, to wait, and to aspire in *silence*, just as all do who have fixed their eyes on this goal. Remember that your truest adviser is to be found, and constantly sought, *within yourself*. Only by experience can you learn to know its voice from that of natural instinct or mere logic, and strengthen this power, by virtue of which the Masters have become what They are.

"Your choice or rejection of this course is the first test of yourself. Others will follow, whether you are aware of them or not, for the first and only right of the neophyte is — *to be tried*. Hence silence and sorrow follow his acceptance instead of the offer of prompt aid for which he looks. Yet even that shall not be wanting; those trials and reverses will come only from the Law to which you have appealed." J. N.

XV

DEAR JASPER:

I gave your letter to a distressed soul: she returned thanks, saying it was a cooling draught to one athirst. The thanks of course are yours. Now this lady says it was refreshment to the weary, that letter. True, or she would not say it. But it was not so to me nor to you.

We needed it not. But she illustrates a certain state of progress. She is not yet where we are; but which is happier? She is happier, but poorer in hope. We are not all too happy, but are rich in hope, knowing the prize at the end of time, and not deterred by the clouds, the storms, the miasms and dreadful beasts of prey that line the road. Let us, then, at the very outset wash out of our souls all desire for reward, all hope that we may attain. For so long as we thus hope and desire, we shall be separated from the Self. If in the Self all things *are*, then we cannot wish to be something which we can only compass by excluding something else.

So being beyond this lady so grateful, we find that everything we meet on this illusory plane of existence is a lure that in one way or another has power to draw us out of our path. That is the point we are at, and we may call it the point where lures of Maya have omnipresent power. Therefore we must beware of the illusions of matter.

Before we got to this stage we knew well the fateful lure, the dazzling mirror of the elemental Self, here and there in well-defined places, and intrenched as it was, so to say, in strongly-marked defenses. Those we assaulted; and that was what it desired, for it did think that it then had no need to exercise the enchantment which is hard because so subtle, and so distributed here and there that we find no citadels to take, no battalions in array. But now our dearest friends are unconsciously in league with the deceptive in nature. How strongly do I realize the dejection of Arjuna as he let his bow drop from his hand and sat down on his chariot in despair. But he had a sure spot to rest upon. He used his own. He had Krishna near, and he might fight on.

So in passing along those stages where the grateful lady and others are, we may perhaps have found one spot we may call our own and possess no other qualification for the task. That spot is enough. It is our belief in the Self, in Masters: it is the little flame of intuition we have allowed to burn, that we have fostered with care.

Then come these dreadful lures. They are, in fact, but mere carcasses, shells of monsters from past existences, offering themselves that we may give them life to terrify us as soon as we have entered them either by fear or love. No matter which way we enter, whether by attachment or by repugnant horror, it is all one: they are in one case vivified by a lover; in the other by a slave who would be free but cannot.

Here it is the lure of enjoyment of natural pleasures, growing out of life's physical basis; there it is self-praise, anger, vanity, what not? Even these beautiful hills and river, they mock one, for they live on untrammelled. Perhaps they do not speak to us because they know the superiority of silence. They laugh with each other at us in the night, amused at the wild struggle of this petty man who would pull the sky down. Ach! God of Heaven! And all the sucklings of Theosophy wish that some great, well-diplomaed Adept would come and open the secret box; but they do not imagine that other students have stepped on the spikes that defend the entrance to the way that leads to the gate of the Path. But we will not blame them, nor yet wish for the things — the special lots — that some of them have abstracted, because now that we know the dreadful power that despair and doubt and violated conscience have, we prefer to prepare wisely and carefully, and not rush in like fools where angels do not pass uninvited.

But, Companion, I remind you of the power of the lure. This Path passes along under a sky and in a clime where every weed grows a yard in the night. It has no discrimination. Thus even after weeks or months of devotion, or years of work, we are surprised at small seeds of vanity or any other thing which would be easily conquered in other years of inattentive life, but which seem now to arise as if helped by some damnable intelligence. This great power of self-illusion is strong enough to create a roaring torrent or a mountain of ice between us and our Masters.

In respect to the question of sex. It is, as you know, given much prominence by both women and men to the detriment of the one sex or the other, or of any supposed sex. There are those who say that the female sex is not to be thought of in the spirit; that all is male. Others say the same for the female. Now both are wrong. In the True there is no sex, and when I said "There all men are women and all women are men," I was only using rhetoric to accentuate the idea that neither one nor the other was predominant, but that the two were coalesced, so to say, into *one*. In the same way you might say, "men are animals there and *vice versâ*." Mind, this is in regard to Spirit, and not in regard to the psychical states. For in the psychical states there are still distinctions, as the psychical, though higher than the material, is not as high as Spirit, for it still partakes of matter. For in the Spirit or Atma *all* experiences of *all* forms of life and death are found at once, and he who is one with the Atma knows the whole manifested Universe at once. I have spoken of this condition before as the Turya or fourth state.

When I say that the female *principle* represents matter, I do not mean *women*, for they in any one or more cases may be full of the masculine principle, and *vice versâ*.

Matter is illusionary and vain, and so the female element is illusionary and vain, as well as tending to the *established order*.* So in the *Kabbala* it is said that the woman is a wall about the man. A balance is necessary, and that balance is found in women, or the woman element. You can easily see that the general tendency of women is to keep things as they are and not to have change. Woman — not here and there women — has never been the pioneer in great reforms. Of

*Through its negative or passive quality. — J. N.

course many single individual women have been, but the tendency of the great mass of the women has always been to keep things as they are until the men have brought about the great change. This is why women always support any established religion, no matter what – Christian, Jewish, Buddhist, or Brahmin. The Buddhist women are as much believers in their religion and adverse from changing it as are their Christian sisters opposed in the mass to changing theirs.

Now as to telling which element predominates in any single person, it is hard to give a general test rule. But perhaps it might be found in whether a person is given to abstract or concrete thought, and similarly whether given to mere superficial things or to deep fundamental matters. But you must work that out, I think, for yourself.

Of course in the spiritual life no organ *disappears*, but we must find out what would be the mode of operation of any organ in its spiritual counterpart. As I understand, the spiritual counterparts of the organs are *powers*, and not organs, as the eye is the power to see, the ear the power to hear, and so on. The generative organs would then become the creative power and perhaps the Will. You must not suppose that in the spirit life the organs are reproduced as we see them.

One instance will suffice. One may see pictures in the astral light through the back of the head or the stomach. In neither place is there any eye, yet we see. It must be by the power of seeing, which in the material body needs the specialized place or specializing organ known as the eye. We hear often through the head without the aid of the auricular apparatus, which shows us that there is the power of hearing and of transmitting and receiving sounds without the aid of an external ear or its inside cerebral apparatus. So of course all these things survive in that way. Any other view is grossly material, leading to a deification of this unreal body, which is only an image of the reality, and a poor one at that.

In thinking over these matters you ought always to keep in mind the three plain distinctions of *physical, psychical, and spiritual, always remembering that the last includes the other two.* All the astral things are of the psychical nature, which is partly material and therefore very deceptive. But all are necessary, for they are, they exist.

The Deity is subject to this law, or rather it is the law of the Deity. The Deity desires experience or self-knowledge, which is only to be attained by stepping, so to say, aside from self. So the Deity produces the manifested universes consisting of matter, psychical nature, and spirit. In the Spirit alone resides the great consciousness of the whole; and so it goes on ever producing and drawing into Itself, accumulating such vast and enormous experiences that the pen falls down at the thought. How can that be put into language? It is impossible, for we at once are met with the thought that the Deity must know all at all times. Yet there is a vastness and an awe-inspiring influence in this thought of the Day and Night of Brahman. It is a thing to be thought over in the secret recesses of the heart, and not for discussion. *It is the All.*

And now, my Brother, for the present I leave you. May your restored health enable you to do more work for the world.

I salute you, my Brother, and wish you to reach the terrace of enlightenment. Z.

Letters That Have Helped Me

Volume II

WILLIAM Q. JUDGE

Letters That Have Helped Me

II

Compiled by
THOMAS GREEN and
JASPER NIEMAND

THEOSOPHICAL UNIVERSITY PRESS
PASADENA, CALIFORNIA

Reprinted from the original edition published in
England in 1905 by Thomas Green.

In Devotion
TO THE IMMORTALS
and in
The Service of Humanity
This little book
is laid
Upon the Altar

June, 1905

Contents

Foreword	ix
Letters	1
Extracts from Letters	52
An Occult Novel	85
William Q. Judge	101

THE MASTER'S LOVE IS BOUNTIFUL; ITS LIGHT SHINES UPON THY FACE AND SHALL MAKE ALL THE CROOKED WAYS STRAIGHT FOR THEE.

Farewell Book

Foreword

ONE marked difference will be noticed between this, the second volume of LETTERS THAT HAVE HELPED ME, and the earlier volume. That first volume had a unity of purpose and development, setting forth, as it did, in due sequence, the salient points of the eastern teaching. This unity palpably arose from the fact that the series of letters was written to one individual, and thus followed along a line suited to the unfolding needs and the studies of that individual, as to those of all fellow students pursuing an identical line of thought.

The present volume, on the contrary, consists of letters, and extracts from letters, written to a number of people in different parts of the world. In many instances, an extract only was sent to the compilers by individuals appealed to, that of their store something might be given to their fellowmen. In other instances, the entire letter was sent, but contained personal or other matter, which could not be published. In still other instances, the entire letter is given. It has been thought best to omit all headings and endings to these letters, in order that no discrimination shall be made in respect of the recipients, thus leaving the truths which the letters embody to stand out in their own relief, unmarred by a label and a name. Many of the extracts were published in *The Irish Theosophist*, and others still in the "Tea-Table" of *The Path*, where "Quickly" stood for Mr. Judge. It was the wish of Mr. Judge, expressed in writing to one of the compilers, that the series should be re-published (with the addition of other matter) as a second volume of the earlier work. The compilers are thus carrying out the direct wishes of Mr. Judge.

During the lifetime of Mr. Judge, it was possible to rearrange, to suggest excision or amplification, or the grouping of various extracts as one letter; and it was possible as well to annotate, since Mr. Judge read all proof, and was always ready to consider any suggestions, while he was also pleased to see that his annotator had grasped his meaning, or to correct errors in this respect. It is evident that such rearrangement, adding as it would to the completeness and the unity of a series, is much to be desired. It was hoped to continue this method with the present volume; but the death of the writer has made it impossible. We can only publish some letters completely, as they stand, and group together such extracts as remain.

One point more. A great number of letters have thus come up. One compiler alone has many score, all written since the publication of the first volume, and ranging over that period of years in which the trials of Mr. Judge became increasingly heavy, a period to which his unexpected death set a term. How great were these trials, none well knew except the Master whom he so devotedly served. The last letter of all was written but a very short while before his death. In no single letter out of all these numbers — in no letters that the compilers have seen — is there a harsh or condemnatory word said of the authors of his trials. He accepts the bitter, the profound injustice done him without one word which could impugn the faith he held, the teachings he gave out. Surprise there is; annoyance once or twice at the waste of time, the irrational deeds and words. And then he turns him to that wise compassion which knows that it is not he who is wronged who is in truth the sufferer, but he who inflicts a wrong.

Mr. Judge always taught the truest Occultism, the highest path. When his hour of trial struck, step by step he followed along that path. In the destiny of the crucified, whether Christs, or Christ-disciples, it is always seen that the loudest denial comes from those most helped, most served. It is he who sits "at meat" with them who betrays them. And of all the long line of martyrs, never one has been exonerated to his era, justified to his age. This fact alone should make thinking men pause, remembering further that the crowd always prefers that Barabbas should be released unto them.

The great drama ever follows the same lines. The initiate, be he disciple or be he adept, cannot defend himself: this is the inexorable law. But he has all the tenderest support that his great predecessors along the path of thorns can bestow: all the joy of a battle nobly fought; all the gratitude of those among his fellows whose intuition can follow him behind the veil which screens the initiate from our sight.

So it comes about that these letters breathe the compassion, the patience, the brotherliness their author lived to inculcate. Sorrow, indeed, he felt; but he put it bravely by. His great and kind heart remained sound to the core. He sweetened the hours of bitterness by profound resignation to The Law. He was one of those of whom it is written: "He that loseth his life for My sake shall find it."

For the helping of mankind we publish these letters. To the judgment of posterity we commit them, knowing well that in the eternal spaces the Truth alone prevails. He who is here seen sustaining and consoling his fellows during the saddest hours of his life and down to the doors of the tomb, was in his turn upheld — not alone by a great faith and by an All-Compassionate Hand — but also by the Love enshrined in his own quiet heart. To the Master he left the rest.

THE COMPILERS

HITHERTO I HAVE BEEN AN EXILE FROM MY TRUE COUNTRY; NOW I RETURN THITHER. DO NOT WEEP FOR ME: I RETURN TO THAT CELESTIAL LAND WHERE EACH GOES IN HIS TURN.

Hermes Trismegistos

Letters

I

DEAR BROTHERS AND SISTERS:

I do not think that you will take it amiss that I again intrude myself before you. I am so far off, and the place where my old friend and teacher — the one who pointed out to me the way that must bring us, if followed, to the light and peace and power of truth — is so dear to me, I would fain speak with those, my fellow-workers, who now live where she worked, and where her mighty soul left the body she used for our advantage. This is surely sufficient reason.

Refer to the Master's letter in *The Occult World* and you will find him saying that the Masters are philanthropists and care only for that. Hence, the very oldest F. T. S. who has been selfish, and not philanthropic, has never come under the notice of the Masters, has never done anything, in fact, toward the development of the soul in his possession, nothing for the race of man. It is not membership in the T. S., or any other mystical body, that brings us near the Masters, but just such philanthropic work with just the pure motive.

Then I know, and say plainly — for as so close to each other we should plainly speak — that some of us, maybe all, have waited and wondered, and wished and hoped, for what? Variously expressed thus: one wants to go to the Master, not knowing even if it be fitting; another wants to know what is the vague longing inside; another says that if the inner senses were but developed and hopes the Master would develop them, and so on; all, however, expressed by what the Master has himself written, "You want to find out about us, of our methods of work, and for that you seek along the line of occultism." Well, it is right for us to seek and to try and to want to reach to Them, for otherwise we never will in any age get where such Beings are. But as wise thinkers we should act and think wisely. I know many of you and what I am saying should help some as it does me also.

You are all on the road to Masters, but as we are now, with the weak and hereditarily diseased bodies we have, we could not live an hour with Masters did we jump suddenly past space to Them. Some too have doubt and darkness, the doubt mostly as to themselves. This should not be harboured, for it is a wile of the lower man striving to keep you back among the mediocre of the race. When you have lifted yourself up over that level of the race, the enemy of man strikes and strives at all times to bring clouds of doubt and despair. You should know that all, everyone, down to the most obscure, who are working steadily, are as steadily creeping on to a change, and yet on and on to other changes, and all steps to the Master. Do not allow discouragement to come in. Time is needed for all growth, and all change, and all development. Let time have her perfect work and do not stop it.

How may it be stopped? How many have thought of this I do not know, but here is a fact. As a sincere student works on, his work makes him come every day near to a step, and if it be an advance then it is certain there is a sort of silence or loneliness all around in the forest of his nature. Then he may stop all by allowing despair to come in with various reasons and pretexts; he may thus throw himself to where he began. This is not arbitrary law but Nature's. It is a law of mind, and the enemies of man take advantage of it for the undoing of the unwary disciple. I would never let the least fear or despair come before me, but if I cannot see the road, nor the goal for the fog, I would simply sit down and wait; I would not allow the fog to make me think no road was there, and that I was not to pass it. The fogs must lift.

What then is the panacea finally, the royal talisman? It is DUTY, Selflessness. Duty persistently followed is the highest yoga, and is better than mantrams or any posture, or any other thing. If you can do no more than duty it will bring you to the goal. And, my dear friends, I can swear it, the Masters are watching us all, and that without fail when we come to the right point and really deserve They manifest to us. At all times I know They help and try to aid us as far as we will let Them.

Why, the Masters are anxious (to use a word of our own) that as many as possible may reach to the state of power and love They are in. Why, then, suppose they help not? As they are Atman and therefore the very law of Karma itself, They are in everything in life, and every phase of our changing days and years. If you will arouse your faith on this line you come nearer to help from Them than you will recognise.

I send you my love and hope, and best thoughts that you may all find the great light shining round you every day. It is there.   Your brother,

WILLIAM Q. JUDGE.

II

ONCE more in the absence of ——— I send you a word of brotherly greeting. I would ask you to read it impersonally in every part, as I have no reserved thoughts and no ulterior aim in it, and have not had any letters or news from anyone to lead me to write. We are so far away from each other that now and then such a greeting is well, and should be taken in the spirit it is sent. It is not possible to send to any other household as none other exists in the Society, you being unique in this, that you are the only one. Here we have no such thing, all nearly living at other places, and this being merely a centre for work.

Many times have co-operative households been tried and failed. One was tried here and is famous. It was called the Brook Farm, but it had no such high aim and philosophy behind it as you have, and thus the personal frictions developed at any place of close intimacy broke it up. That should be a guide to you to enable you to watch and avoid. Yours may alter in number and in *personnel*, but can never really be broken up if the aim is high and the self-judgment is strict and not self-righteous. I am not accusing you of this, but only stating a common human danger, from which the Theosophist is not at any time exempt. Indeed, he is in danger in your centre from the fact that strong force revolves around it. Hence all must be ever careful, for the personal element is one that ever has a tendency to delude us as it hides behind various walls and clothes itself in the faults, real or imaginary, of *others*.

Your centre being the only one as yet of such size, it is useful to think how you may best all act as to make it truly international. Each one has a right to his or her particular "crank," of course, but no one ought to think that anyone else is to be judged from not being of the same stripe of "crank." One eats meat, another does not. Neither is universally right, for the kingdom of heaven does not come from meat, or from its absence. Another smokes and another does not; these are neither universally right nor wrong, as smoke for one is good and for another is bad; the true cosmopolitan allows each to do in such matters as he likes. Essentials are the only things on which true occultism and Theosophy require an agreement, and such temporary matters as food and other habitual daily things are not essentials. One may make a mistake, too, of parading too much his or her particular line of life or act. When this is done the whole world is bored, and nothing effective or lasting is gained except a cranky impression.

In a place like yours, where so many of all sorts of nature are together, there is a unique opportunity for gain and good in the chance it gives one for self-discipline. There friction of personality is inevitable, and if each one learns the great "give and take," and looks not for the faults of the others but for the faults he sees in himself, because of the friction, then great progress can be made. The Masters have said that the great step is to learn how to get out of the rut each one has by nature and by training, and to fill up the old grooves. This has been misconstrued by some who have applied it to mere outer habits of life, and forgotten that its real application is to the mental grooves and the astral ones also. Each mind has a groove, and is not naturally willing to run in the natural groove of another mind. Hence comes often friction and wrangle. Illustrate it by the flanged wheel of the steam-engine running on a track. It cannot run off nor on a track of broader or narrower gauge, and so is confined to one. Take off the flange and make the face of the wheel broader, and then it can run on any road that is at all possible. General human nature is like the engine, it is flanged and run for a certain size of track, but the occultist or the would-be one should take off the flange and have a broad-faced wheel that will accommodate itself to the other mind and nature. Thus in one life even we might have the benefit of many, for the lives of other men are lived beside us unnoticed and unused because we are too broad and flanged in wheel, or too narrow and flanged also. This is not easy, it is true, to change, but there is no better opportunity than is hourly presented to you in the whole world, to make the alteration. I would gladly have such a chance, which Karma has denied me, and I see the loss I incur each day by not having it there or here. You have it, and from there should go out to all the earth soon or late, men and women who are broad and free and strong for the work of helping the world. My reminding you of all this is not a criticism, but is due to my own want of such an opportunity, and being at a distance I can get a clearer view of the case, and what you have for your own benefit and also for all others.

It is natural for one to ask: "What of the future, and what of the defined object, if any, for our work?" That can be answered in many ways.

There is, first, our own work, in and on ourselves, each one. That has for its object the enlightenment of oneself for the good of others. If that is pursued selfishly some enlightenment comes, but not the amount needed for the whole work. We have to watch ourselves so as to make of each a centre from which, in our measure, may flow out the potentialities for good that from the adept come in large and affluent streams. The future then, for each, will come from each present moment. As we use the moment so we shift the future up or down for good or ill; for the future being only a word for the present — not yet come — we have to see to the present more than all. If the present is full of doubt or vacillation, so will be the future; if full of confidence, calmness, hope, courage and intelligence, thus also will be the future.

As to the broader scope of the work, that comes from united effort of the whole mass of units. It embraces the race, and as we cannot escape from the destiny of the race we have to dismiss doubt and continue at work. The race is, as a whole, in a transition state, and many of its units are kept back by the condition of the whole. We find the path difficult because, being of the race, the general race tendencies very strongly affect us. This we cannot do away with in a moment. It is useless to groan over it: it is also selfish, since we, in the distant past, had a hand in making it what it now is. The only way we can alter it is by such action now as makes of each one a centre for good, a force that makes "for righteousness," and that is guided by wisdom. From the great power of the general badness we each one have a greater fight to wage the moment we force our inner nature up beyond the dead level of the world. So before we attempt that forcing we should, on the lower plane, accumulate all that we can of merit by unselfish acts, by kind thoughts, by detaching our minds from the allurements of the world. This will not throw us out of the world, but will make us free from the great force which is called by Boehme the "Turba," by which he meant the immense power of the unconscious and material basis of our nature. That material base being devoid of soul is more inclined on this plane to the lower things of life than to the higher.

Hence, until we have in some degree conquered that, it is useless for us to be wishing, as so many of us do, to see the Masters and to be with Them. They could not help us unless we furnish the conditions, and a mere desire is not the needed condition. The new condition calls for a change in thought and nature.

So the Masters have said this is a transition age, and he who has ears to hear will hear what has thus been said. We are working for the new cycles and centuries. What we do now in this transition age will be like what the great Dhyan Chohans did in the transition point — the midway point — in evolution at the time when all matter and all types were in a transition and fluid state. They then gave the new impulse for the new types, which resulted later in the vast varieties of nature. In the mental development we are now at the same point: and what we now do in faith and hope for others and for ourselves will result similarly on the plane to which it is all directed. Thus in other centuries we will come out again and go on with it. If we neglect it now, so much the worse for us then. Hence we are not working for some definite organisation of the new years to come, but for a change in the Manas and Buddhi of the Race. That is why it may seem indefinite, but it is, nevertheless, very defined and very great in scope. Let me refer you to that part of *The Secret Doctrine*, penned by Master Himself, where the midway point of evolution is explained in reference to the ungulate mammals. It should give you a glimpse of what we have to do, and remove all vain longings for a present sojourn with our unseen guides and brothers. The world is not free from superstition, and we, a part of it, must have some traces left of the same thing. They have said that a great shadow follows all innovations in the life of humanity; the wise one will not bring on that shadow too soon and not until some light is ready to fall at the same time for breaking up the darkness.

Masters could give now all the light and knowledge

needed, but there is too much darkness that would swallow up all the light, except for a few bright souls, and then a greater darkness would come on. Many of us could not grasp nor understand all that might be given, and to us would result a danger and new difficulty for other lives, to be worked out in pain and sorrow. It is from kindness and love that Masters do not blind us with the electric flash of truth complete.

But concretely there is a certain object for our general work. It is to start up a new force, a new current in the world, whereby great and long-gone Gnanis, or wise ones, will be attracted back to incarnate among men here and there, and thus bring back the true life and the true practices. Just now a pall of darkness is over all that no Gnani will be attracted by. Here and there a few beams strike through this. Even in India it is dark, for there, where the truth is hid, the thick veil of theological dogma hides all; and though there is a great hope in it the Masters cannot pierce through to minds below. We have to educate the West so that it may appreciate the possibilities of the East, and thus on the waiting structure in the East may be built up a new order of things for the benefit of the whole. We have, each one of us, to make ourselves a centre of light; a picture gallery from which shall be projected on the astral light such scenes, such influences, such thoughts, as may influence many for good, shall thus arouse a new current, and then finally result in drawing back the great and the good from other spheres from beyond the earth. This is not spiritualism at all, for it has no reference to the denizens of spook-land in any way.

Let us then have great faith and confidence. See how many have gone out from time to time from your centre to many and distant parts of the world, and how many will continue to go for the good and the gain of man of all places. They have gone to all parts, and it must be that even if the centre should be disrupted from causes outside of you, its power and reality will not be destroyed at all, but will ever remain, even after all of it may have gone as far as bricks and mortar are concerned.

I give you my best wishes and brotherly greeting for the new year and for every year that is to come.

Affectionately yours,

WILLIAM Q. JUDGE.

III

I SEND you this, and you will keep it, using it later on when I give the word. It is to be headed by me later.

The Theosophical movement was begun as a work of the Brotherhood of which H. P. B. is a member, and in which the great Initiate, who was by her called Master, is one of the Chiefs.

It was started among Western people by Western people, the two chief agents being H. P. B., a Russian, and H. S. Olcott, an American. The place where it was started was also Western — the City of New York.

But notwithstanding that the Brotherhood thus had it begun, it must, as a Society, be kept with a free platform, while, at the same time, its members are individually free to take and hold what belief they find approved by conscience, provided that belief does not militate against Universal Brotherhood. Hence they are at perfect liberty to believe in the Lodge of that Brotherhood and in its messengers, and also to accept their doctrines as to man, his nature, powers, and destiny as given out by the messengers on behalf of the Lodge.

The fact is significant that the Theosophical movement was thus, as said, begun in the Western world, in the country where the preparations for the new root race are going on, and where that new root is to appear. This was not to give precedence to any one race or country over another, or to reduce any race or country, but was and is according to the law of cycles, which is a part of evolution. In the eye of that great Law no country is first or last, new or old, high or low, but each at the right time is appropriate for whatever the work is that must be performed. Each country is bound up with all the others and must assist them.

This movement has, among others, an object which should be borne in mind. It is the union of the West with the East, the revival in the East of those greatnesses which once were hers, the development in the West of that Occultism which is appropriate for it, so that it may, in its turn, hold out a helping hand to those of older blood who may have become fixed in one idea, or degraded in spirituality.

For many centuries this union has been worked towards and workers have been sent out through the West to lay the foundations. But not until 1875 could a wide public effort be made, and then the Theosophical Society came into existence because the times were ripe and the workers ready.

Organisations, like men, may fall into ruts or grooves of mental and psychic action, which, once established, are difficult to obliterate. To prevent those ruts or grooves in the Theosophical movement, its guardians provided that necessary shocks should now and then interpose so as to conduce to solidarity, to give strength such as the oak obtains from buffetting the storm, and in order that all grooves of mind, act, or thought, might be filled up.

It is not the desire of the Brotherhood that those members

of the Theosophical movement who have, under their rights, taken up a belief in the messengers and the message should become pilgrims to India. To arouse that thought was not the work nor the wish of H. P. B. Nor is it the desire of the Lodge to have members think that Eastern methods are to be followed, Eastern habits adopted, or the present East made the model or the goal. The West has its own work and its duty, its own life and development. Those it should perform, aspire to and follow, and not try to run to other fields where the duties of other men are to be performed. If the task of raising the spirituality of India, now degraded and almost suffocated, were easy, and if thus easily raised could it shine into and enlighten the whole world of the West, then, indeed, were the time wasted in beginning in the West, when a shorter and quicker way existed in the older land. But in fact it is more difficult to make an entry into the hearts and minds of people who, through much lapse of time in fixed metaphysical dogmatism, have built, in the psychic and psycho-mental planes, a hard impervious shell around themselves, than it is to make that entry with Westerners who, although they may be meat eaters, yet have no fixed opinions deep laid in a foundation of mysticism and buttressed with a pride inherited from the past.

The new era of Western Occultism definitely began in 1875 with the efforts of that noble woman who abandoned the body of that day not long ago. This does not mean that the Western Occultism is to be something wholly different from and opposed to what so many know, or think they know, as Eastern Occultism. It is to be the Western side of the one great whole of which the true Eastern is the other half. It has, as its mission, largely entrusted to the hands of the Theosophical Society, to furnish to the West that which it can never get from the East; to push forward and raise high on the circular path of evolution now rolling West, the light that lighteth every man who cometh into the world — the light of the true self, who is the one true Master for every human being; all other Masters are but servants of that true One; in it all real Lodges have their union.

Woe is set apart — not by Masters but by Nature's laws — for those who, having started in the path with the aid of H. P. B. shall in any way try to belittle her and her work, still, as yet not understood and by many misunderstood. This does not mean that a mere person is to be slavishly followed. But to explain her away, to belittle her, to imagine vain explanations with which to do away with what is not liked in that which she said, is to violate the ideal, is to spit back in the face of the teacher through whom the knowledge and the opportunity came, to befoul the river which brought you sweet waters. She was and is one of those servants of the universal Lodge sent to the West to take up the work, well knowing of the pain and obloquy and the insult to the very soul — worst of all insults — which were certain from the first to be hers. "Those who cannot understand her had best not try to explain her: those who do not find themselves strong enough for the task she plainly outlined from the beginning had best not attempt it." She knew, and you have been told before, that high and wise servants of the Lodge have remained with the West since many centuries for the purpose of helping it on to its mission and destiny. That work it would be well for the members of the Theosophical movement to continue without deviating, without excitement, without running to extremes, without imagining that Truth is a matter of either longitude or latitude: the truth of the soul's life is in no special quarter of the compass, it is everywhere round the whole circle, and those who look in one quarter will not find it.

(This letter is marked in red pencil, by the hand of Mr. Judge, "unfinished." In fact, it ends with the word "will," as above, but in publishing earlier some extracts from this letter, the owner had the permission of the writer to supply the last three words, which he had intended to place there when called away, and in his haste for the post, in returning, had omitted to add.)

IV

TO THE THEOSOPHICAL PUBLICATION SOCIETY:

It is with great regret that I learn from recent London advices that the Managers of the Society there think that the Tract, "Epitome of Theosophy," which appeared in *The Path*, is "too advanced to be reprinted now, and that what is needed is 'a stepping-stone from fiction to philosophy.'"

Permit me to say that I cannot agree with this opinion, nor with the policy which is outlined by it. The opinion is erroneous, and the policy is weak as well as being out of accord with that of the Masters. Those Masters have approved the project of the new Society and are watching the unfolding of its policy.

If I had made up that Epitome wholly myself I might have some hesitation in speaking in this way, but I did not. The general idea of such a series of tracts was given to me some two years ago, and this one was prepared by several students who know what the people need. It is at once comprehensive and fundamental. It covers most of the ground, and if any sincere reader grasps it he will have food for his reflection of the sort needed.

If, however, we are to proceed by a mollified passage from folly (which is fiction) to philosophy, then we at once diverge from the path marked out for us by the Masters; and for this statement I can refer to letters from Them in my hands. I need only draw your attention to the fact that when those Masters began to cause Their servants to give out matter in India, They did not begin with fiction, but with stern facts such as are to be found in the *Fragments of Occult Truth*, which afterwards became Mr. Sinnett's *Esoteric Buddhism*. We are not seeking to cater to a lot of fiction readers and curiosity hunters, but to the pressing needs of earnest minds. Fiction readers never influenced a nation's progress. And these earnest minds do not desire, and ought not to be treated to a gruel which the sentence just quoted would seem to indicate as their fate.

Then again, I beg to remind my English brothers in this enterprise that they should remember that the United States contain more theosophists and possible subscribers and readers than the whole of Europe. They do not want fiction. They want no padding in their search for truth. They are perfectly able to grasp that which you call "too advanced." The Master some years ago said that the U. S. needed the help of the English body of theosophists. That they did not get, and now do not require it so much, and their ideas and needs must be considered by us. We have twenty-one Branches to your three in Great Britain, and each month, nearly, sees a new Branch. Several have written me that they understand the T. P. S. is to give them *good* and *valuable* reprints and not weak matters of fiction.

I therefore respectfully urge upon you that the weak and erroneous policy to which I have referred shall not be followed, but that strong lines of action be taken, and that we leave fiction to the writers who profit by it or who think that thus people's minds can be turned to the Truth. If a contrary line be adopted then we will not only disappoint the Master (if that be possible) but we will in a very large sense be guilty of making false representations to a growing body of subscribers here as well as elsewhere.

I am, Fraternally Yours,
WILLIAM Q. JUDGE.

V

It is a relief to turn from these eternal legal quibbles (of my business) to say a word or two on eternal matters.

Now and then there are underlined sentences occurring in *The Path*. These ought to be studied. One about one yogee not doing anything not seen in another yogee's mind will open up a subject. Reticence does not always mean ignorance: if we dig out the knowledge we drag down at the same time rocks and debris of other sorts, whereas, if a miner hands us the nugget, that is all we get at the time. So a slight reticence often results in our going at the digging ourselves.

In September *Path* is another. Getting back the memory of other lives is really the whole of the process, and if some people don't understand certain things it is either because they have not got to that point in their other lives or because no glimmer of memory has yet come.

The communion of saints is a reality, and it often happens that those brought up in the same school speak the same language. While not being one, such are very like co-scholars no matter when or where. Furthermore, there are some peculiar natures in this world who, while they are like mirrors or sponges that reflect and absorb from others certain information, still retain a very strong individuality of their own. So it is with this gentleman whose letter you enclose. There is scarcely any doubt that he, if he tells true tales, sees in the astral light. The description of things "moving about like fishes in the sea" is a real description of one of the manners in which many of these elemental forms are seen. So it may, as premised above, be settled that he sees in the astral light.

He should know that that astral light exists in all places and interpenetrates everything, and is not simply in the free air alone. Further should he know that to be able to see as he sees in the light is not *all* of the seeing thus. That is, there are many sorts of such sight, *e.g.*, he may see now certain airy shapes and yet not see many others which at the same time are as really present there as those he now sees. So it would seem that there are "layers" or differences of states in the astral light. Another way to state it is that elementals are constantly moving in the astral light — that is, everywhere. They, so to say, show pictures to him who looks, and the pictures they show will depend in great part upon the seer's thoughts, motives and development. These differences are very numerous. It therefore follows that in this study *pride* must be eliminated. That pride has disappeared from ordinary life does not prove that it has done any more than retreat a little further within. So one must be careful of becoming even inwardly vain of being able to see any such things; for if that happens it will follow that the one limited plane in which one may be a seer will be accepted as the whole. That, then, will be falsity. But if recognised as delusive because partial, then it remains true — so far as it goes. All true things must be total, and all totalities exist at once, each in all, while these partial forms exist partially in those that are total. So it follows that only those that are total reveal entire truth, and those that partake of lower nature — or are partial — receive but a limited view of truth. The elementals are partial forms, while the man's individual soul is total, and according to the power and purity of that form which it inhabits "waits upon the Gods."

Now our bodies, and all "false I" powers up to the individual soul, are "partial forms" in common with the energic centres in astral light. So that it must follow that no matter how much we and they participate in each other the resulting view of the one Truth is partial in its nature because the two partial forms mingling together do not produce totality. But it intoxicates. And herein lies the danger of the teaching of such men as P. B. Randolph, who advocates participation with these partial beings by means of sensual excesses glorified with a name and gilded with the pretence of a high purpose — *viz.*, knowledge: KNOWLEDGE MUST BE CAREFULLY OBTAINED WITH A PURE MOTIVE.

This motive is the point for this gentleman to study. He says that he "will know," and that he "desires to escape from present limitations of this personality, which is all loneliness."

As he did go forward on the path of knowledge, he would find that this imaginary loneliness of which he speaks is by comparison with the utter loneliness of that path, a howling mob, a tramping regiment.

As he is fighting alone his own fight let him carefully note his motive in seeking to know more, and in seeking to escape from his present "loneliness." Must it not be true that loneliness cannot be escaped from by abhorrence of it or even by its acceptance, but by its recognition? What next? Well, this; and perhaps it is too simple. He ought to assure himself that his motive in knowing and being is that he may help all creatures. I do not say that this is not now his motive, but for fear it should not be I refer to it. For as he appears to be on the borderland of fearful sights and sounds he ought to know the magic amulet which alone can protect him while he is ignorant. It is that boundless charity of love which led Buddha to say: "Let the sins of this dark age fall on me that the world may be saved," and not a desire for escape or for knowledge. It is expressed in the words: "THE FIRST STEP IN TRUE MAGIC IS DEVOTION TO THE INTERESTS OF OTHERS." It was expressed by Krishna when he said: "Near to Renunciation is salvation" (or the state of a Jivanmukta).

But he naturally will ask if he should cultivate his powers. Well, of course he should at some time or other; but he ought to begin at motive and purification of thought. He may, if he chooses, abandon the ideas of this large-hearted charity and yet make great progress in "powers," but surely then death and ashes will be the result. That does not concern me.

Why did he have a "horror" when he merely succeeded in going away from his body; in being for a moment free? That is an important question. Its solution may be found in many ways. I will mention one. If the place, or person he wished to go to was one to which he then ought not to have gone — or if his motive in desiring to go there was not pure — then a horror might result that drove him back. But if even with a bad motive he had attempted to go to a place where a similar motive existed, then no horror would have come. If he will tell himself, or me, just where he was wanting to go, I may say why he had a horror. But I do not want to know.

For it is not necessarily a horror-producing thing to leave the body. Only lately I know of a friend of mine who went out of his body a distance of 10,000 miles and had no horror. In that case he desired to see a friend on a common purpose which had in view the amelioration of this dark age; and again, who left his body in the country and saw the surrounding sweeps of wood and vale and had no horror whatever in either case.

If one is sure of motive, and that is pure, then going out of the body is not detrimental.

An illustration will show the dangers. Take the case of one who is able to leave the body and who determines to go to one who is sympathetic. The second one, however, is protected by high motive and great purity: the first is mixed in motive in waking life, which, as soon as the other disengaged state comes on, changes into a mere curiosity to see the second, and perhaps with more or less sensuality, *e.g.*, a desire to see a woman much admired and to pour into her unwilling ear pretended or real human love. The elementals (and so on) of the second protect that soul and hurl vague horrors at the first who, if he is not a skilled black magician is:

1. Either merely pushed back into the body; or
2. Is assailed with fears that prevent him finding his body, and that may be occupied by an elementary, good, bad, or indifferent — and his friends may say that he waked up insane!

Well; enough!

VI

THE letters proposed by your friend are a device of the enemy, as you may have supposed, and which you were warned to expect in unexpected quarters and ways. Therefore they should not be written. It is the small rift in the lute that destroys it; in human history small and unexpected events alter the destinies of nations.

On this plane the dark powers rely upon their ability to create a maya. They have seen that you are not to be trapped in the prominent lines of work and so try their hands where your currents exist in a prominent place but with a very small matter. Let me point out.

If you issue these letters they would be an endorsement of all that your friend might think to do, and neither you nor Y. are free from mistakes yet. They would amount to a declaration, to the perception of others, that you were guiding Y. in everything and were at all times conscious of it. Do you or Y. know where this would end? Do you see the possibilities flowing from the acceptance in full of those letters by the others? And what would their action be? Are they free from the curse of superstition; are they clear in the co-ordination of psychic with brain thought? No. The result would not only be different from what you and Y. can see, but worse. Now further.

It is true — and humanly natural — that the others (like you and *your* friends) indulged in some slight critiques on your friend, but they were small and coupled with sincere and kind thoughts up to their lights, no matter how large and bitter all this was made by maya to appear. The dark powers seized on them, enlarged them, dressed them up, assumed the images of the thinkers, enlivened the thoughts with elementals, all with an object, *viz.*, to make your friend think it all came from the others. Why, if that were so then those others (poor, weak mortals) are friends. But are they? No. It was wished by the dark ones to irritate your friend, and you, so as, by the irritation, to split a breach forever unhealable. In Y.'s very weak state they found it easy, and hoped by distance to make you blind.

Tell your friend to remember what was long ago said; that the Master would manage results. You must not manage, precipitate, nor force. Beware. Let Y. assume that the others do not think harshly nor critically, but put it all against the dark powers, and the results will be managed by Master. As chelas and students conceal rather than give out your inner psychic life, for by telling of it your proper progress is hindered. There must be silence in heaven for a time or the dark ones rejoice to so easily get good, malleable images for annoying you. It will be tried again either that way or some other. By gentleness, detachment, strict attention to duty, and retiring now and then to the quiet place bring up good currents and keep back all evil ones. Remember it is the little things the work is done through, for they are not noticed, while the larger ones draw the eyes and minds of all.

I think of you always as the brave soldier, made not of mud and soft things, but made of long pieces of steel and strips of diamond and flashes of long light that has no harshness, and a big, big spring all the way through. That is you. And your eyes laugh now and then, even if you do have a pain in your head. Inside you are all right, as you know very well, don't you? Then if you are that soldier, it means that he will spring back as soon as the body has had time to get some better. The body is like the heart; it has to have time to get to some other condition. But you will get there. A steady mind and heart stands still and quiet until the muddy stream rolls clear. Now sleep, I say; I command you to sleep. I have tried to help you to sleep, and I wish you to sleep, for sleep will do you good as nothing else can.

I hope to see you drop all when ——— comes, and go to sleep for awhile, and far enough from the row to be quiet. It is sleep your tired nature on the outside wants, for sleep knits up the ravelled thread of life and makes us young again. You have been so awake, that the power of equilibrium between life and the body is disturbed and needs a chance. This is fact. One can get wrought up, and then Prana is too strong; so little children sleep much. *Be a child once.*

Well, I'm near home, or rather the centre spot, for pilgrims like you and I have no real house and don't want it; it's too dull and usual for such to want a home. And perhaps the little brother is good and well? He shall be ever present, as he always has been, in those little songs and tales told to oneself in the dark, and is, too, the lone warrior seen on the plain of stupid infantry, and he rides a horse whose blood is electricity. Au revoir. Tell ——— I can stand alone; it is the best way to stand, and what I always was and shall be. Let the ripples and the foam go on coming and going; the old river and the bed of the river do not move for all that is on the top. Is it not so? Well, good-bye, and good luck, and may the devas help you and also karma. Love to all, as usual.

As forevermore,

VII

I was very glad indeed to get your letter, but sorry to read of your troubles. Strangely, too, a similar trouble with a very dear friend of mine is now uppermost in my mind, and I would like to crave the favour from you that you would tell me what kind of place the asylum is you speak of. The only accessible one here is a mere prison, where men do nothing, and where I do not think the influence would be other than depressing. Do you think that the one you have in mind, a man of active mind, who merely wishes to get rid of his present trouble, would be able to occupy himself?

I am indeed sorry that you have to tell me such matters, but they will rest in my confidence; and I thank you and ———— for your renewed invitation.

It is best not to inquire into some of the mysteries of life, but surely a full reliance upon the Spirit within and upon the law that the hands that smite us are our own, will relieve the pressure of some events that seem mysteries. I find the greatest consolation in these reflections, and then I see that each moment is mine, and that when gone it is passed and merged into the sum of my being: and so I must strive to Be. Thus I may hope to become in time the conscious possessor of the whole of Being. So I do not strive after mystery. The great struggle must be to open up my outer self, that my higher being may shine through, for I know that in my heart the God sits patient, and that his pure rays are merely veiled from me by the many strivings and illusions that I bring on outwardly. This being so, I can only look at the Society and its work (under my lights) as the best available channel for my actions in the effort to help others. Its methods, then, as far as I am concerned, will be only mine, and thus I cannot attach to it the methods of any other person. Believe me sincerely yours,

VIII

As for me, all that is the matter is my health, not yet full and good. If that were all right, I would have nothing. What do I care for all the row? It will soon be over; some will be dead; the sooner the better, and then we shall have other fun. I look at it all as so much fun and variety, sure; I am not joking. It is variety, and without that what would life be? As all these asses bray we learn new notes of the scale not known before. A heap of letters I got; but I am O. K., fragile, perhaps, but not brittle. I would like to be with you both and have some sweet fun without tears or spite, but we have to be apart, to meet now and then. Poor ———! Don't be hard on him. He had to be silent, you know. A small matter, but more important than he knew for him. Let up on him, and don't jeer. He has a hard time enough with himself, to have any added by massage from others.

C———'s allusion to "suffering" opens up a vein of thought which I have had. I have examined myself for the "uses" of this rumpus, to see if I am properly "suffering." Well, I can't find it. Down in the deeps I may be; but I find myself cheerful, happy, and anything but morose or sad. Ergo: can I be suffering? Do you know? Positively, I do not know. Ought I? Am I a wretch because I do not suffer, or because, being in actual suffering, I am insensate and do not perceive it? But, on the other hand, I feel no anger and no resentment. Really, it puzzleth me. Many nights I do not sleep, and have used the hours (as I now do), when all is still, in looking over all, and yet I feel all right — everywhere. Of course, I have committed my human faults and sins, but I mean, on the Grand Round-Up, I find nothing to "suffer me"; nothing that I shall rush out to amend by taking the ridiculous and nasty world to my bosom in confidence upon.

As for myself. Well. What? Nothing. I know not and care not. I am joyful and glorious that the work thus goes. My desires are not here, and all the racket sounds to me far off, as if miles from my ear. I am acting as a pump-engine, and trying to force a lot on. This is not for myself. I must find myself alone, as we all are, and then the Law will say: "Next!" But what next I do not care and don't want to know, for when "Next" is said I will see what it is to do. Just now the best and biggest work by us poor children is on this plane with the great aid of Master, Whose simple single will keeps the whole organisation, and acts as its support and shield. We are not big enough yet to handle the Akasa, but we may help Them to, and that is all I want to do. I have used the present affairs to be as a lesson to me, for it may be used as a test to me as to pride and ambition; and I find that, no matter how I turn it, the same result comes. I am seeking other things while working in this. Try as I may to raise an ambition for power, and to raise a desire to change a supposed case (non-existent in fact), I can't do it. So you see, my dear Comrade, I am all right.

These questions you ask me:

When the Self is first seen it is like looking into a glove; and for how many incarnations may it not be so? The material envelope throws up before the eye of the Soul waving fumes and clouds of illusion.

The brain is only the focus through which the forces and thoughts are centralised that are continually coming in through the solar plexus of the heart. Many such thoughts, therefore, are lost, just as millions of seeds in nature are lost. It behooves to study them and to guard them when there; but can we call them our own? Or weep over them? Let us be as wide as great Nature concerning them, and let each go on to its own place without colouring them with our own colour and acceptance or adhesion.

The spiral movement is the double movement of the astral light, one spiral inside the other. The diastole and systole of the heart are caused by that double movement of the Akasa. But do not presumptuously grasp the movement too soon, for often even the heart moving too rapidly destroys the life.

The brutes unconsciously are aware of the general human opposition, which in each human being they see focalized.

It is easier to sink back into the Eternal than to dive. The diver must needs have the power to retain breath against the rush caused by diving, while to sink gives time to get and keep the breath.

Nothing else greatly new. Am waiting to hear of your completer health. Sustained on the wave you will come in with the tide in time. Best love to ——— and to ——— and to thee. May you all be well sustained. I think I have now given you all there is. Salute most noble, brave, and diamond-hearted! May we meet after the dust settles, and we will meet forever in the long, long manvantaras before us all. Peace! Peace! the path of peace and not of war: such are the words.   As forevermore,

IX

I DO not know what to write, for I've been so occupied with people. I am anxious about my lectures; still unprepared. I cannot naturally reply to many of your points, because I have a retiring feeling, and so shall not reply. Indeed, I often think how nice it would be not to speak or write. I am no hand at those nice phrases that people like.

Of course, that does not alter my real feelings, but chickens are chickens and often think nonsense. I want to forget and forgive all those children and childish acts. Let us do it, and try as much as possible to be real brothers, and thus get nearer the truth. And by work we will defeat the enemy of Master: by still silently working.

I hope still you will emerge sooner or later all the better and the stronger. I know you will and I do not see you dead by any means. You are less hopeful for yourself than for others. But you have the will and the fire to fight on to the last bone and the last moment. I only wish I could see you all to hearten you up a little more: that is, to talk with you, for you do not need much of the grit. . . .

I often hear from Him now. That terrible racket cleared me up. He says that much haste must be avoided. And that I must not let the flood carry me off. He asks me to say to you that you have a natural rapidity that must be guided by yourself and the best way is to wait after a letter and to sleep on a plan. He also says that . . . (I am not aware of this, but He must be right), that you have a subtle desire to be the first to make or propose a good plan or act. Do not let this carry you off, but be slower as to that. It is good advice, I think, for the additional reason that one can now and then take a plan from the head of another.

I see the clans have been gathering. Keep it up and see to it as far as possible that partisanship is at a low ebb and that only good, steady loyalty and work are the main motive. *And cast no one out of your heart.*

I must ask for a calmer motion at this time. It is absolutely necessary.

A word of love to ———— ? I sent it. I sent many. I

not only sent it visible but also the other way. What could I say? I do not know. In what I sent my whole heart was put. Does not ———— forever stand for me and with me? How can I use words when the fibres of my heart are involved? And what good is my philosophy if, when the actual taking of ———— off seemed so near, I indulged in mere words? I cannot do it. If I try, then the words are mere rubbish, lies and unreal, as I am not able to do this, no matter how much others can. Our real life is not in words of love or hate or coldness but in the fiery depths of the heart. And in those depths ———— is and was. Could I say more? No; impossible. And even that is small and badly said.

It is true that day by day the effect of my philosophy is more apparent on me, as yours is and will be on you, and so with us all. I see it myself, let alone all I hear of it from others. What a world and what a life! Yet we are born alone and must die alone, except that in the Eternal Space all are one, and the One Reality never dies.

If ambition creeps up slowly higher and higher it will destroy all things, for the foundations will be weak. In the end, the Master will win, so let us breathe deep and hold fast there, as we are. And let us hurry nothing. Eternity is here all the time. I cannot tell you how my heart turns to you all. You know this, but a single word will do it. *Trust!* That was what H. P. B. said. Did she not know? Who is greater than our old and valiant "old Lady"? Ah, were she here, what a carnage! Wonder, anyhow, how she, or he, or it, looks at the matter? Smiling, I suppose, at all our struggles.

Again, in storm and shine, in heat and cold, near or afar, among friends or foes, the same in One Work.

X

My Dear Companion (Campanero),

Your long letter and message received. All I can say is that it is gigantically splendid, marvellously accurate. And let me then return to you this message . . . that this must prove to you that you are not standing still. . . . It's all well enough to be out in the rapids as you say I am, but what of it when I don't hear such a message as yours myself? Thank you. It is a bugle blast from the past. Perhaps in some other age I taught you that and now you give it to me again. When I said in mine that in Kali Yuga more could be done than in any other age in the same period, I stated all you say but I didn't know it. Now your clear light falls upon it and I see it well. But fear not. You got so familiar to me that I permitted myself to let out some of the things that I now and then feel. But I swear to you that I do not let them always so rush before me. Truly you have proved that your place is "where the long roll finds you standing."

Now don't you begin to see more and more things? Don't you feel things that you know without anyone to tell you?

My friend Urban has shown me a letter from ——— in which the latter, feeling dark in consequence of various causes, sees no light. This is merely the slough of despond, I tell him. We know the light is ahead, and the experience of others shows that the darkest hour is just before the dawn. I tell him also that strong souls are thus tried inevitably because they rush ahead along the road to the light. In the *Finnish Epic* it is said that guarding a certain place are hideous serpents and glittering spears. And so it really is.

But although such is the truth, I have also to tell him

that he ought, as far as possible, to try to ameliorate the circumstances. I will make my meaning clear. He is living now, as you know, among people of an opposite faith. Around them are elementals who would, if they could, implant suspicion and distrust about those whom he reveres, or, if they fail there, will try to cause physical ills or aggravate present ones. In his case these have succeeded in part in causing darkness. . . . Now ———, while not just in that case, is surrounded, while not strong, by those who inwardly deplore his beliefs . . . and hence the elementals are there and they quarrel with those of ——— and bring on despair, reduce strength, and so on. I tell ——— those circumstances ought to be ameliorated every now and then: for I know he would at once, if changed to a better place, get better. And so I have written to him to make a change as soon as he can.

It is highly important that no replies should be made to attacks. Get the people to devote themselves to work and to ignoring attacks. The opposing forces strain every nerve to irritate some or all of us so that we may reply in irritation and precipitate more follies. Consider solely how to improve old work, get up new work and infuse energy into work. Otherwise the beneficent influences intended for all F. T. S. will be nullified.

Cheer up ———, and from your standpoint tell him how to know the distinction between the intellect and spiritual mind. Tell him how to find out his spirit-will and to ignore a little the mental attitude he takes. Do not point to particular instances of his own failure but detail your own inner experience. It will do him good.

Upanishads. "Subsisting" here means, not that the self *exists* by reason of food, but that as a manifestation, as one causing the body to be visible and to act, the self subsists in that state by means of the food which is used. It is really a reversed translation, and ought to read — as I think — "The self exists in close proximity to the heart and causes the body to exist by reason of the food which it takes in for its subsistence." That is, continual reference is had to the doctrine that if the self were not there the body would not exist. Yes: it also means that the self procures vital airs from the food which the one life causes to be digested. For note that which you know, that did we not take food the material unit of the trinity would die and the self be disappointed, and then would get another body to try in again. For is it not permitted to each one to try and set up a habit in that material unit whereby we may as incarnated beings know the self? Then when that is done we do not live as others; but all the same, even then, the self must subsist, so to say, while in manifestation, by means of food, no matter if that food be of a different character, corresponding to the new state. Even the Devas subsist by food. You know "they enter into that colour, or sound, or savour, at the sacrifice, they rise in that colour, etc., and by it they live." Watch words, ——— dear; they are traps. Catch ideas and I will understand you by the context that you are not confined to the ordinary meanings.

I am swamped in work, but my courage is up, and I feel the help sent from the right place.

Let us go on from place to place and from year to year; no matter who or what claims us outwardly, we are each the property of the self.

As forevermore and after,

XI

To ———.

There is a sentence in your letter not explained by J. Niemand, which, however, needs explaining, for it is the outgrowth of an erroneous idea in you. You say: "Can I help these ignorant elementals with mental instruction? I tried it, but not successfully."

In all those cases where it is caused by the elementals you *cannot*. Elementals are not ignorant. They know just as little and just as much as you do. Most generally more. Do you not know that they are reflectors? They merely mirror to you either your own mind, or [the] mental strata caused by the age, the race, and the nation you may be in. Their action is invariably automatic and unconscious. They care not for what is called by you "mental instruction." They hear you not.

Do you know how they hear, or what language they understand? Not human speech; nor ordinary human thought clothed in mental speech. That is a dead letter to them altogether.

They can only be communicated with through correlations of colours and sounds. But while you address yourself to them, those thoughts assume life from elementals rushing in and attaching themselves to those thoughts.

Do not, then, try to speak to them too much, because did you make them know they might demand of you some boon or privilege, or become attached to you, since in order to make them understand they must *know* you, and a photographic plate forgets not.

Fear them not, nor recoil in horror nor repulsion. The time of trial must be fulfilled. Job had to wait his period until all his troubles and diseases passed away. *Before* that time he could do naught.

But we are not to idly sit and repine; we are to bear these trials, meanwhile drawing new and good elementals so as to have — in western phrase — a capital on which to draw when the time of trial has fully passed away.

On all other points Niemand has well explained. Read both together.

Lastly; know this law, written on the walls of the temple of learning.

"Having received, freely give; having once devoted your life in thought, to the great stream of energy in which elementals and souls alike are carried — and which causes the pulse beat of our hearts — you can never claim it back again. Seek, then, that mental devotion which strains to give. For in the law it is written that we must give away all or we lose it: as you need mental help, so do others who are wandering in darkness seeking for light."

XIII*

To-day I got your wire, "——— very low." This is a shock to me. I hardly believe it is the end at all. I cannot believe it, there is so much fire there. But I wired you to ask if I was to tell ———. Also to read 2nd ch. *Bhag. Gîtâ.* That, my dear fellow, solves all these troubles for me though it don't kill out immediate pain. Besides, it is Karma just and wise. Defects are in us all, and if this is the taking off why it means that a lot of obstructive Karma is thus at once and for ever worked off, and has left ——— free for greater work in better places. I would I were there with you. Tell him how much I love him and that in this era of Kali Yuga

[*Apparently misnumbered in original edition.]

no sincere one, such as he, remains long away from the work there is to do. Words are of no use. I have sent thoughts, and those are useful, whether we are in the body or out of it. I sent every night lately all the help I could and continued through the day, not only to ———, but also to you. It reached there, I know, but I can't overcome Karma if it is too strong.

Tell ——— if it should come to the worst, that no regrets about the work are needed. What has already been accomplished there will last, and seethe, and do its work for several years to come. So in that direction there could be nothing to regret. I cannot write ——— directly: but if able to hear this — or maybe when it arrives — then head it as if it were to him, and not to you.

So, dear ———, in the presence of your wire this is all I can write. You know my feelings, and I need not say any more. As Ever,

XIV

You did right to send me that letter. Of course, I am sorry to hear from you in that way, but am glad that you wrote. Let me tell you something — will you believe it? You are not in nearly such a bad way as you think, and your letter, which you sent me unreservedly, shews it. Can you not, from the ordinary standpoint of worldly wisdom, see it so? For your letter shews this; a mind and lower nature in a whirl, not in the ordinary sense, but as though, figuratively speaking, it were whirling in a narrow circle, seemingly dead, kept alive by its own motion. And above it a human soul, not in any hurry, but waiting for its hour to strike. And I tell you that I know it will strike.

If so far as your personal consciousness goes you have lost all desire for progress, for service, for the inner life — what has that to do with it? Do you not think that others have had to go through with all of that and worse; a positive aversion, may be, with everything connected with Theosophy? Do you not know that it takes a nature with some strength in it to sink very low, and that the mere fact of having the power to sink low may mean that the same person in time may rise to a proportionately greater height? That is not the highest path to go but it is one that many have to tread. The highest is that which goes with little variation, but few are strong enough to keep up the never ceasing strain. Time alone can give them that strength and many ages of service. But meanwhile there is that other to be travelled. Travel it bravely.

You have got the ———, which of the hells do you think you are in? Try to find out and look at the corresponding heaven. It is very near. And I do not say this to bolster you up artificially, for that would be of no use and would not last, even if I were to succeed in doing it. I write of facts and I think that somewhere in your nature you are quite well aware that I do so.

Now what is to be done: * * * * In my opinion you should deliberately give yourself a year's trial. Write and tell me at the end of that year (and meantime as often as you feel called upon to do so, which will not be very often) how you then feel, and if you do not feel inclined to go on and stick to it I will help you all I can. But you must do it yourself, in spite of not wanting to do it. You can.

Make up your mind that in some part of your nature somewhere there is that which desires to be of use to the world. Intellectually realise that that world is not too well off and probably wants a helping hand. Recognise mentally that you should try to work for it sooner or later. Admit to yourself that another part of your nature — and if possible see that it is the lower part — does not care in the least about the world or its future, but that such care and interest should be cultivated. This cultivation will of course take time: all cultivation does. Begin by degrees. Assert constantly to yourself that you intend to work and that you will do so. Keep that up all the time. Do not put any time limit to it, but take up the attitude that you are working towards that end. Begin by doing ten minutes' work every day of any sort, study, or the addressing of envelopes, or anything, so long as it be done deliberately and with that object in view. If a day comes when this is too irksome, knock it off for that day. Give yourself three or four days' rest and do it deliberately. Then go back to your ten minutes' work. At the end of six or seven weeks you will know what to add to that practice: but go slowly, do nothing in a hurry, be deliberate.

Don't try to feel more friendly to this or that person — more actively friendly I should have said. Such things must spring up of their own accord and will do so in time. But do not feel surprised that you feel *all* compassion die out of you in some ways. That too is an old story. It is all right because it does not last. Do not be too anxious to get results from the practice I have outlined above. Do not look for any: you have no concern with them if you do all that as a duty. And finally, do not forget, my dear fellow, that the dead do come to life and that the coldest thing in the world may be made hot by gentle friction. So I wish you luck, and wish I could do more for you. But I will do what I can.

XV

Now this is, as I said, an era. I called it that of Western Occultism, but you may give it any name you like. But it is western. The symbol is the well-intended American Republic, which was seen by Tom Paine beforehand "as a new era in the affairs of the world." It was meant as near as possible to be a brotherhood of nations, and that is the drift of its declaration and constitution. The T. S. is meant to be the same, but has for many years been in a state of friction. It has now, if possible, to come out of that. It cannot be a brotherhood unless each, or some, of its units becomes a brother in truth. And *brother* was the noble name given in 1875 to the Masters. Hence you and I and all of us must cultivate that. We must forgive our enemies and those who assail us, for only thus can the great brothers properly help by working through us. There seems to be a good deal to forgive, but it is easily done inasmuch as in fifty years we'll all be gone and forgot.

Cut off, then, thoughts about those "foolish children" until harmonious vibrations ensue to some extent. That absurdity . . . let go. I have deliberately refrained from jumping at such a grand chance. So you see forgive, forgive and largely forget. Come along, then, and with me get up as fast as possible the feeling of brotherhood.

Now then, you want more light, and this is what you must do. You will have to "give up" something. To wit: have yourself called half an hour earlier than is usual and devote it *before* breakfast to silent meditation, in which brood upon all great and high ideas. Half an hour! Surely that you can spare. And don't eat first. If you can take another half *before* you go to bed and without any preliminaries of undressing and making things agreeable or more comfortable, meditate again. Now don't fail me in this. This is much to give up, but give it up, recollecting that you are not to make all those preparations indulged in by people.... "The best and most important teacher is one's seventh principle centred in the sixth. The more you divest yourself of the illusionary sense of personal isolation, and the more you are devoted to the service of others, the more Maya disappears and the nearer you approach to Divinity." Good-bye, then, and may you find that peace that comes from the self.

XVI

IN answer to your questions:

(1) Clothes and astral form.

Answer. – You are incorrect in assuming that clothes have no astral form. Everything in nature has its double on other planes, the facts being that nothing visible in matter or space could be produced without such a basis. The clothes are seen as well as the person because they exist on the astral plane as well as he. Besides this, the reason why people are seen on the astral plane with clothes of various cut and colour, is because of the thought and desire of the person, which clothes him thus. Hence a person may be seen in the astral light wearing there a suit of clothes utterly unlike what he has on, because his thought and desire were on another suit, more comfortable, more appropriate, or what not.

(2) What can true and earnest Theosophists do against the Black Age or Kali Yuga?

Answer. – Nothing *against* it but a great deal *in* it; for it is to be remembered that the very fact of its being the iron or foundation age gives opportunities obtained in no other. It is only a quarter as long as the longest of the other ages, and it is therefore crammed four times as full of life and activity. Hence the rapidity with which all things come to pass in it. A very slight cause produces gigantic effects. To aspire ever so little now will bring about greater and more lasting effects for good than at any other time. And similarly evil intent has greater powers for evil. These great forces are visibly increased at the close of certain cycles in the Kali Yuga. The present cycle, which closes Nov. 17th, 1897 — Feb. 18th, 1898, is one of the most important of any that have been. Opportunities for producing permanent effects for good in themselves and in the world as a whole, are given to Theosophists at the present time, which they may never have again if these are scattered.

XVII

THE Masters have written that we are all bound together in one living whole. Hence the thoughts and acts of one react upon all.

Experience has shewn that it is true, as said by Masters, that any sincere member in any town can help the T. S. and benefit his fellow townsmen. It is not high learning that is needed, but solely devotion to humanity, faith in Masters, in the Higher Self, a comprehension of the fundamental truths of Theosophy and a little, only a little, sincere attempt to present those fundamental truths to a people who are in desperate need of them. That attempt should be continuous. No vain striving to preach or prove phenomena will be of any value, for, as again Masters have written, one phenomenon demands another and another.

What the people want is a practical solution of the troubles besetting us, and that solution you have in Theosophy. Will you not try to give it to them more and more and save ——— from the slough it is in?

I would distinctly draw your attention to Brother ———. There is not that complete sympathy and toleration between him and you there ought to be, and for the sake of the work it should be otherwise. You may say that it is his fault. It is not wholly, for you must also be somewhat to blame, if not in this life then from another past one. Can you deny that for a long period he has held up the Branch there? for if he had not it would have died out, even though you also were necessary agents.

Have any of you had unkind or revengeful feelings to him? If so, ought you not to at once drive them out of your hearts. For I swear to you on my life that if you have been troubled or unfortunate it is by the reaction from such or similar thoughts about him or others. Drive them all out of your hearts, and present such kindliness and brotherliness to him that he shall, by the force of your living kindness, be drawn into full unity and co-operation with you.

Discussion or proofs to shew that you are all right and he wrong avail nothing. We are none of us ever in the right, there is always that in us that causes another to offend. The only discussion should be to the end that you may find out how to present to the world in your district, one simple, solid, united front.

As to the expression "seeing sounds," this you understand, of course, so far as the statement goes. It records the fact that at one time the vibrations which cause a sound now were then capable of making a picture, and this they do yet on the astral plane.

XVIII

In reply to your question:

Neither the general law nor the Lodge interferes to neutralise the effect of strain upon the disciple's physical energies when caused by undue exertion or want of regularity, except in certain cases. Hence the Theosophist is bound to see that his arrangement of hours for sleep, work and recreation are properly arranged and adjusted, as he has no right to so live as to break himself down, and thus deprive the cause he works for of a useful and necessary instrument.

Your friend's energies have been disarranged and somewhat exhausted by irregularities as to rest and recreation, since work has been hard and required rest — whether asleep or awake — has not been had. This causes excitement, which will (or has) react in many different ways in the system and upon the organs. It causes mental excitement which again raises other disturbance. He, like anyone else, should take measures so as to insure regularity as to rest, so that what work he does shall be better and the present excitement subside in the system. It is not wise to remain up late unless for good purposes, and it is not that to merely remain with others to late hours when nothing good or necessary can be accomplished. Besides other reasons, that is a good one.

Excitement is heat; if heat be applied to heat, more is produced. Coolness must be applied so as to create an equilibrium. This applies in that case, and the establishment of regularity in the matter of rest is the application of coolness. Second, the various exciting and "wrongful" acts or thoughts of others are heat; coolness is to be produced by discharging the mind of those and ceasing to refer to them in words, otherwise the engendered heat will continue. It is needless to refer to reasons resting on the points of conduct and example, for those anyone is capable of finding and applying.

As there is no hurry, it is easy to divest the mind of anxiety and the irritation arising from hurry. Again, comparison of one's work or ways of doing things better than others is wrong and also productive of the heat above spoken of.

XIX

You are right in thinking that the essential principles of Theosophy are often stated without the use of that name, for it is the only universal fundamental system which underlies the religions of every age. The New Testament, rightly understood, teaches Theosophy, and we know that both Jesus and St. Paul were initiates. Of course, in Theosophy, as in any other Science, one understands more as one reads more, and I recommend you to read and digest such of our books as you can conveniently procure.

Now in respect to the questions you ask, let me say that Theosophy requires no man to abandon a mode of life which is not in itself wrong. The use of meat diet is not a sin; it is not even an offence; it is a habit which the race has now largely conformed to, and is not a question of morals or right. At a certain stage of advance as a chela or disciple, the use of meat food has to be abandoned because of its psychical and physiological effects. But you have not reached that stage, nor is it likely that you will for a long time. As the use of meat is not an offence, so neither can be the supply of it to others, so that your assisting in killing hogs for market is in no way opposed to your duty as a man or as a

Theosophist. That being your duty in present circumstances, I should recommend you to perform it without hesitation.

Men and women are complementary in character, and therefore adapted to each other. It is natural that each sex should enjoy the company of the other, and what is natural cannot be wrong. Moreover, it is perfectly proper that when a suitable mate is found a man should marry and settle down as a householder, bringing up a family with right views and high purposes. He contributes a service to humanity, who puts to take his place after his death, children who reproduce his true and altruistic life. Consequently, if you find a suitable match and desire matrimony, there can be no possible reason why you should not carry out such a purpose. Like the abstention from meat, celibacy is essential to advance after a certain stage, but that stage has not yet been reached by you, and you cannot, therefore, be subjected to its conditions. There can be no one rule laid down for all human beings, inasmuch as the temperaments and desires are so different. Each must work out the problem of life in his own way. If your aspirations are so set on higher things that you find the lower a hindrance, it is evident that you should not indulge in the latter; but if you are not so hindered, then no less a duty is yours. You are right in thinking that the essential to all true progress is a wish to conform utterly to the Divine Will, we being certain that we shall be helped in proportion, as is our need.

XX

YES, you are right. I am in danger, but that danger is not on the outside, although it is on the outside that attempts are brought forward. And in some sense all those with me are in danger too. It is a danger from ———— which ever tries to forestall the steps of those who travel forward. So too, my Dear, you are in the same sort of danger. But while the danger is there, yet there is encouragement in the fact itself. For we would not be so placed if we had not been so fortunate as to have progressed through work and patience to the point where ——— sees enough in us to try and stop progress and hinder our work. Hence, if they see they cannot stop us, they try all plans to get up strife, so as to nullify our work. But we will win, for knowing the danger we take measures against it. I am determined not to fail. Others may; but ——— and I will not. Let us then await all suffering with confidence and hope. The very fact that you suffer so much is objective evidence of progress, even though so painful, not only to you but to those who love you. So while I do not say "suffer on," I am comforted by the knowledge that it will be for great good in the future. So I am writing this, instead of machining it, in order that you may feel the force of my love and comradeship.

Let us all draw closer together in mind and heart, soul and act, and try thus to make that true brotherhood through which alone our universal and particular progress can come.

To thee, oh holder of the flame, my love I send. Well, I go again, but never do I forget. My best love and blessing to thee. I cannot speak of these things, but thou knowest.

And now, as formerly, and as now, and as forever and forevermore.

XXI

Doubts and questions have arisen as to some things since the present cloud gathered. Among others it has been said that it were better that ——— had left the chair: it would be well for him to go, and so on. These views should not be held. If held, they should be dismissed. There are two forces at work in the T. S., as well as in the world and in man. These are the good and the bad. We cannot help this: it is the Law. But we have rules, and we have preached of love and truth and kindness; and above all, we have spoken of gratitude, not only of Masters, but among us. Now this applies to this question of ———. Again, he may be incompetent . . . and yet be competent for the little he has to do. . . . Now let me tell you: the work must not fail because here and there personalities fall, and sin, and are unwise. TRUTH remains, and IT IS, whoever falls: but the multitude look to the visible leader. If he falls apart like an unjointed puzzle, at once they say, "there is no truth there, nothing which IS": and the work of a century is ruined and must be rebuilt again from its foundations, and years of backward tendency must come between the wreck of one undertaking and the beginning of another. Let me say one thing I KNOW: only the feeling of true brotherhood, of true love towards humanity aroused in the soul of someone strong enough to stem this tide, can carry us through. For LOVE and TRUST are the only weapons that can overcome the REAL enemies against which the true theosophist must fight. If I, or you, go into this battle from pride, from self-will, from desire to hold our position in the face of the world, from anything but the purest motives, we shall fail. Let us search ourselves well and look at it as we never looked before: see if there is in us the reality of the brotherhood which we preach and which we are supposed to represent.

Let us remember those famous words: "Be ye wise as serpents and harmless as doves." Let us remember the teaching of the Sages that death in the performance of our duty is preferable to the doing by us of the duty of another, however well we may do the latter: the duty of another is full of danger. Let us be of and for peace, and not for war alone.

XXII

It is true ——— suffered through my cold and hard feelings. But it was her fault, for I say now as then to ——— that she, absorbed in ———, neglected my members, who are my children, and for whom I wanted her best and got her worst. That made me cold, of course, and I had to fight it, and didn't care if ——— did not like it: I have no time to care. I am glad she has gone to ———. It is her trial and her chance and when she gets back she can see for herself if she is able to prevent the "big head" from coming on as has happened with others. If she does, then she will have stood the reaction and I have faith she will stand; but still it has to be met. Time comes on sure, and with it trial. H. P. B. was her preparer and comfort, but men are not made into steel by comfort, and note that H. P. B. then died off.

My trip all over this country shows me that it is of more consequence that I should now work up the U. S., where the Masters first worked in this century. It needs all I can do. . . . So when I have fulfilled my engagement on the English stage I shall skip back here quickly and do this work. The field is even greater than I thought, although I had a big idea of it. From the United States we can affect the world and they will come to us from all places either for solid work or for help in their need. . . .

Well now, of you: I feel it all. It is up, and down. It is well you are courageous, and to endure you are able. Indeed endure is the best word, for that is what the oak does when the storms rage, for it is better to endure when we can do nothing than to faint and fall. The facts are to be faced. I hope they may turn out otherwise, but if not, it is karma. Aside from pain, it is the same as anything else. If it comes, it will not last long. Still, I hope it cometh not. I think much of it, but know the bravery of you and the high soul that dwells there. All the time of pain and dogged fighting I know your real self sits up above it all unaffected, and so does mine, and from that let us take comfort. All things in this age move like lightning and so with all our karma, though mine has so often seemed slow, so far as concerns me. Well, I cannot go on with this: I feel as you do: I stand by you in heart and have often of late sent you messages of hope and power to help you.

I advised ——— to do her part to lessening the constant bringing forward of the name of H. P. B., instead of independent thought on Theosophy. We have too much of it and it is no proof of loyalty, and it gives rise to much of the foolish talk of our dogmatism. You will understand, and may be able to influence some to a more moderate though firm attitude that will not lessen their loyalty and devotion. One good point is that the true chela does not talk much of his Master and often does not refer to that Master's existence. It has almost become the same as unnecessarily waving the red flag to a bull. Those of us who have experience do not do it; but the younger ones do. X——— does it here in his speeches and I am going to speak to him of it. If it be not avoided the first thing we know there will be a split between the H. P. B.'ers and the theosophists *pur sang*, the latter claiming to be the real thing because devoid of any personal element. You and I and ——— do not find it necessary all the time to be flinging her (H. P. B.) in the faces of others, and it is well now to take the warning offered from the outside. Besides, I have had a very strong inside warning on it. My best love now that we are near Christmas and New Year, and may there be some sunshine to light the path. I send you my love unsullied by a mere gift.

I hope ——— will be firm and proceed as indicated, but she, like us all, must meet her own old enemies in herself.

Again I go, as for evermore.

XXIII

GREAT excitement last night. It was the regular night of ——— T. S. and ——— was to speak. We got there at 8.15, and it was full. He began and had just been fifteen minutes when it was discovered that the building was on fire. We stopped and let 1,000 people in the various halls get out, then quietly went and none were hurt, only two, ——— and ———, getting a few quarts of water from a burst hose.

It was a queer exit, for we went downstairs beside the elevator, and glass, bricks and water were falling down the light well, while the fire on the top stories of it roared and made a fine light, and streams of fire ran down the oily elevator pipes on the other side; and firemen pulled up hose neck or nothing as we got away. It was ———'s own meeting, and it ended in fire! None of the great psychics present had had the remotest premonition, but one invented afterwards an *ex post facto* sense of terror.

Tell ——— the time has passed for him to vacillate; he knows his guru: she was and is H. P. B.; let him reflect ere he does that which, in wrecking her life and fame, will wreck his own life by leaving him where nothing that is true may be seen. . . . Silence is useful now and then, but silence sometimes is a thing that speaks too loud. I am his friend and will help. No one can hurt him but himself; his work and sacrifice were noble and none can point at him.

See what I said in the opening vol. of *The Path:* that the study of what is now called "practical occultism" was not the object of that journal. "We regard it as incidental to the journey along the path. The traveller, in going from one city to another, has perhaps to cross several rivers; maybe his conveyance fails him and he is obliged to swim, or he must, in order to pass a great mountain, know engineering in order to tunnel through it, or is compelled to exercise the art of locating his exact position by observation of the sun: but all that is only incidental to his main object of reaching his destination. We admit the existence of hidden, powerful forces in nature, and believe that every day greater progress is made towards an understanding of them. Astral body formation, clairvoyance, looking into the astral light, and controlling elementals is all possible, but not all profitable. The electrical current, which when resisted in the carbon produces intense light, may be brought into existence by any ignoramus who has the key to the engine-room and can turn the crank that starts the dynamo, but is unable to prevent his fellow man or himself from being instantly killed, should that current accidentally be diverted through his body. The control of these hidden forces is not easily obtained, nor can phenomena be produced without danger, and in our view the attainment of true wisdom is not by means of phenomena, but through the development which begins within. True occultism is clearly set forth in the *Bhagavad-Gita* and *Light on the Path*, where sufficient stress is laid upon practical occultism, but after all, Krishna says, the kingly science and the kingly mystery is devotion to and study of the light which comes from within. The very first step in true mysticism and true occultism is to try and apprehend the meaning of Universal Brotherhood, without which the very highest progress in the practice of magic turns to ashes in the mouth.

"We appeal, therefore, to all who wish to raise themselves and their fellow creatures — man and beast — out of the thoughtless jog-trot of selfish everyday life. It is not thought that Utopia can be established in a day: but through the spreading of the idea of Universal Brotherhood, the truth in all things may be discovered. What is wanted is true knowledge of the spiritual condition of man, his aim and destiny. Such a study leads us to accept the utterance of Prajapati to his sons: 'Be restrained, be liberal, be merciful,' it is the death of selfishness."

This is the line for us to take and to persevere in, that all may in time obtain the true light.

THE LIGHT OF THE EYE FADETH, THE HEARING LEAVETH THE EAR, BUT THE POWER TO SEE AND TO HEAR NEVER DESERTETH THE IMMORTAL BEING, WHICH LIVETH FOREVER UNTOUCHED AND UNDIMINISHED.
— *Book of Items*

Extracts

XXIV

On Theosophy and the T. S.

ALL the work that any of us do anywhere redounds to the interest and benefit of the whole T. S., and for that reason we know that we are united.

The Self is one and all-powerful, but it must happen to the seeker from time to time that he or she shall feel the strangeness of new conditions; this is not a cause for fear. If the mind is kept intent on the Self and not diverted from it, and comes to see the Self in all things, no matter what, then fear should pass away in time. I would therefore advise you to study and meditate over the *Bhagavat Gita*, which is a book that has done me more good than all others in the whole range of books, and is the one that can be studied all the time.

This will do more good than anything, if the great teachings are silently assimilated and put into action, for it goes to the very root of things and gives the true philosophy of life.

If you try to put into practice what in your inner life you hold to be right, you will be more ready to receive helpful thoughts and the inner life will grow more real. I hope with you that your home may become a strong centre of work for Theosophy.

You want to know the inner situation of the T. S., well, it is just this: we have all worked along for eighteen years, and the T. S. as a body has its karma as well as each one in it. Those in it who have worked hard, of course, have their own karma, and have brought themselves to a point ahead of the T. S. Now, if the branches are weak in their knowledge of Theosophy, and in their practice of its precepts and their understanding of the whole thing, the body is in the situation of the child who has been growing too fast for its strength, and if that be the case it is bound to have a check. For my part I do not want any great rush, since I too well know how weak even those long in it are. As to individuals, say you, . . . and so on. By reason of hard and independent work you have got yourselves in the inner realm just where you may soon begin to get the attention of the Black Magicians, who then begin to try to knock you out, so beware. Attempts will be silently made to arouse irritation, and to increase it where it now exists. So the only thing to do is to live as much as possible in the higher nature, and each one to crush out the small and trifling ebullitions of the lower nature which ordinarily are overlooked, and thus strength is gained in the whole nature, and the efforts of the enemy made nil. This is of the highest importance, and if not attended to it will be sad. This is what I had in view in all the letters I have sent to you and others. I hope you will be able to catch hold of men, here and there, who will take the right, true, solid view, and be left thus behind you as good men and good agents.

―――

When I was in ――― I broached to you and others the plan of getting Theosophy to the working people. Has anything been done? It must be simply put. It can be understood. It is important. Let us see if this thing cannot be done; you all promised to go to work at it. Why not turn, like the Bible man, to the byways and hedges from all these people who will not come? Then I feel sure that, if managed right, a lot of people who believe in Theosophy but don't want to come out for it, would help such a movement, seeing that it would involve talking to the poor and giving them sensible stuff. If need be, I'd hold a meeting every night, and not give them abstractions. Add music, if possible, etc. Now let me hear your ideas. Time rolls on and many queer social changes are on the way.

I have your long letter from ——— and you are right as to conduct of Branches. No Branch should depend on one person, for, if so, it will slump, sure; nor on two or three either. Here they depended on me for a long time, and my bad health in voice for a year was a good thing as it made the others come forward. ——— is right enough in his way, but certainly he ought to be fitting himself for something in addition to speaking, as the T. S. has to have a head as well as a tongue; and if a man knows he is bad at business, he should mortify himself by making himself learn it, and thus get good discipline. We sadly need at all places some true enthusiasts. But all that will come in time. The main thing is for the members to study and know Theosophy, for if they do not know it how can they give any of it to others? Of course, at all times most of the work falls upon the few, as is always the case, but effort should be made, as you say, to bring out other material.

. . . . I am abundantly sure that you are quite correct in saying that it is the Branches which work that flourish, and that those addicted to "Parlour Talks" soon squabble and dwindle. You have gone right to the root of the matter. So, also, I agree with you, heart and soul, in what you say as to the policy of a timid holding and setting forth of Theosophy. Nothing can be gained by such a policy, and all experience points to energy and decision as essential to any real advance.

You are, I think, quite right to attempt to get all members to work for their individual advance, by working for their Branches. By doing things in this way, they provide an additional safeguard for themselves, while forming a centre from which Theosophical thought can radiate out to help and encourage others who are only beginning their upward way.

I find that you state my view exactly. That view is that the A B C of Theosophy should be taught all the time, and this not only for the sake of outsiders, but also for the sake of the members who are, I very well know, not so far along as to need the elaborate work all the time. And it is just because the members are not well grounded that they are not able themselves to get in more inquirers. Just as you say, if the simple truths practically applied as found in Theosophy are presented, you will catch at last some of the best people, real workers and valuable members. And Theosophy can best be presented in a simple form by one who has mastered the elements as well as "the nature of the Absolute." It is just this floating in the clouds which sometimes prevents a Branch from getting on. And I fully agree, also, that if the policy I have referred to should result temporarily in throwing off some few persons it would be a benefit, for you would find others coming to take their places. And I can agree with you, furthermore, out of actual experience.

You by no means need to apologise for asking my attention to the matter of your joining the Theosophical Society. It is my great desire and privilege to give to all sincere enquirers whatever information I may possess, and certainly there can be no greater pleasure than to further the internal progress of any real student and aspirant. I think you quite right in wishing to identify yourself with the Theosophical Society, not only because that is the natural and obvious step for anyone sincerely interested; but also because each additional member with right spirit strengthens the body for its career and work.

In taking advantage of an opportunity to introduce Theosophy into the secular press you are doing exactly the work which is so invaluable to the Society, and which I so constantly urge upon our members. It is in this way that so very many persons are reached who would otherwise be quite inaccessible, and the amount of good which seed thus sown can accomplish is beyond our comprehension. You have my very hearty approval of and encouragement in your work and I am very sure that that work will not be without fruit.

NEW YORK, *October 11th*, 1892. — This is the era of *Western Occultism.* We are now to stand shoulder to shoulder in the U.S. to present it and enlarge it in view of coming cussedness, attacks which will be in the line of trying to impose solely Eastern disciples on us. The Masters are not Eastern or Western, but universal.

I shall be glad to give you any information possible respecting Theosophy and the Theosophical Society, but I think you err in supposing that the purpose of either is to encourage the study of what is known as the Occult Arts. Knowledge concerning, and control of, the finer forces of nature are not things which should be sought after at our elementary stage of progress, nor would such attainment be appropriate, even if possible, to anyone who had not thoroughly mastered the principles of Theosophy itself.

Mere desire for powers is a form of selfishness, and receives no encouragement from our Teachers. Mme. Blavatsky stated this matter very clearly indeed in an article published in *Lucifer*, entitled "Occultism *versus* the Occult Arts." When persons without a large preliminary training in the real Wisdom-Religion seek knowledge on the Occult plane they are very apt, from inexperience and inadequate culture, to drift into black magic. I have no power to put you into communication with any adept to guide you in a course of Occult study, nor would it be of service to you if the thing was possible. The Theosophical Society was not established for any such purpose, nor could anyone receive instructions from an adept until he was ripe for it. In other words, he must undergo a long preliminary training in knowledge, self-control, and the subjugation of the lower nature before he would be in any way fit for instruction on the higher planes. What I recommend you to do is to study the elementary principles of Theosophy and gain some idea of your own nature as a human being and as an individual, but drop entirely all ambition for knowledge or power which would be inappropriate to your present stage, and to correct your whole conception of Theosophy and Occultism.

XXV

On Masters

I THINK the way for all western theosophists is through H. P. B. I mean that as she is the T. S. incarnate, its mother and guardian, its creator, the Karmic laws would naturally provide that all who drew this life through her belonged to her, and if they denied her, they need not hope to reach . . . : for how can they deny her who gave this doctrine to the western world? They share her Karma to little purpose, if they think they can get round this identification and benefit, and . . . want no better proof that a man does not comprehend their philosophy. This would, of course, bar him from . . . by natural laws (of growth). I do not mean that in the ordinary business sense she must forward their applications or their merits; I mean that they who do not understand the basic mutual relation, who undervalue *her* gift and *her* creation, have not imbibed the teaching and cannot assimilate its benefits.

She must be understood as being what she is to the T. S., or Karma (the law of compensation, or of cause and effect) is not understood, or the first laws of occultism. People ought to *think* of this: we are too much given to supposing that events are chances, or have no connection with ourselves: each event is an effect of the Law.

What should be done is to realise that "the Master-Soul is one" with all that that implies; to know the meaning of the old teaching, "Thou art That." When this is done we may with impunity identify our consciousness with that of anything in nature; not before. But to do this is a lifetime's work, and beforehand we have to exhaust all Karma, which means duty; we must live for others and then we will find out all we *should* know, not what we would *like* to know.

Devotion and aspiration will, and do, help to bring about a proper attitude of mind, and to raise the student to a higher plane, and also they secure for the student help which is unseen by him, for devotion and aspiration put the student into a condition in which aid can be given to him, though he may, as yet, be unconscious of it. But conscious communication with one's Master can only be accomplished after *long* training and study. What a student has to do, and is able to do, is to fit himself to receive this training.

The recognition from a Guru will come when you are ready, and my advice to you is that, if possible, you put away from yourself the desire for such recognition; for such desire will hinder you. If you will read the *Bhagavat Gîtâ*, especially chapters ii. and iii., I think you will find much to help you. There it says: "Let, then, the motive for action be in the action itself, not in the event. Do not be incited to actions by the hope of their reward . . . perform thy duty . . . and laying aside all desire for any benefit to thyself from action, make the event equal to thee, whether it be success or failure." It is but natural that a student should hope for recognition from a Master, but this desire is to be put aside, and that work is to be done which lies before each. At the same time each one knows that the effect follows the cause, hence whatever our due, we shall receive it at the right time.

―――――

Every Chela (and we are all that once we determine to be) has these same difficulties. Patience and fortitude! For an easy birth is not always a good one. The kingdom of heaven is only taken by violence, and not by weakness of attack. Your constant aspiration persevered in in secret has led you to that point where just these troubles come to all. Console yourself with the thought that others have been in the same place and have lived through it by patience and fortitude. . . . Fix your thoughts again on Those Elder Brothers, work for Them, serve Them, and They will help through the right appropriate means and no other. To meditate on the Higher Self is difficult. Seek then, the bridge, the Masters. "Seek the truth by strong search," by doing service, and by enquiry, and Those who know the Truth will teach it. Give up doubt, and arise in your place with patience and fortitude. Let the warrior fight, the gentle yet fierce Krishna, who, when he finds thee as his disciple and his friend, will tell thee the truth and lighten up the darkness with the lamp of spiritual knowledge.

―――――

Attacks cannot hurt, they must needs come, but all we have to do is to keep right on, working steadily, and Masters will see after the rest. For, that which is done in Their name will come right; and this whole thing has arisen because I have chosen to proclaim my personal belief in the existence of these beings of grandeur. So, let us shake again with the confidence born from the knowledge of the wisdom of the Unseen Leaders, and we go forth separately once more, again to the work, if even not to meet until another incarnation is ours. But meeting then, we shall be all the stronger for having kept faith now.

———

I am glad that you have such a faith in the Great Workers who are behind us. They *are* behind us, to my personal knowledge, and not behind me only, but behind all sincere workers. I know that their desire is that each should listen to the voice of his inner self and not depend too much on outside people, whether they be Masters, Eastern disciples or what not. By a dependence of that kind you become at last thoroughly independent, and then the unseen helpers are able to help all the more.

———

We are all human and thus weak and sinful. In that respect in which we are better than others, they are better than we are in some other way. We would be self-righteous to judge others by our own standard. . . . Are we so wise as never to act foolishly? Not at all. . . . Indeed I have come to the conclusion that in this nineteenth century a pledge is no good, because everyone reserves to himself the right to break it if he finds after a while that it is galling, or that it puts him in some inconsistent attitude with something he may have said or done at some other time . . . In ———'s case, . . . everyone should never think but the very best, no matter what the evidences are. Why, if the Masters were to judge us exactly as They must know we are, then good-bye at once. We would all be sent packing. But

Masters deal kindly with us in the face of greater knowledge of our thoughts and evil thoughts from which none are yet exempt. This is my view, and you will please me much if you will be able to turn into the same, and to spread it among those on the inside who have it not. It is easy to do well by those we like, it is our duty to make ourselves do and think well by those we do not like. Masters say we think in grooves, and but few have the courage to fill those up and go on other lines. Let us who are willing to make the attempt try to fill up these grooves, and make new and better ones.

———

... Keep up your courage, faith and charity. *Those who can to any extent assimilate the Master, to that extent they are the representatives of the Master, and have the help of the Lodge in its work.* ... Bear up, firm heart, be strong, be bold and kind, and spread your strength and boldness.

———

H. P. B. then said that it is by falling and by failing that we learn, and we cannot hope at once to be great and wise and wholly strong. She and the Masters behind expected this from all of us; she and They never desired any of us to work blindly, but only desired that we work unitedly.

———

H. P. B. wrote me in 1890: "Be more charitable for others than for yourself, and more severe on yourself than on others." This is good advice. A strain always weakens the fibres and produces friction. I hope all misunderstandings will fly away.

XXVI

On Occult Philosophy

BEGIN by trying to conquer the habit, almost universal, of pushing yourself forward. This arises from personality. Do not monopolise the conversation. Keep in the background. If someone begins to tell you about himself and his doings, do not take first chance to tell him about yourself, but listen to him and talk solely to bring him out. And when he has finished suppress in yourself the desire to tell about yourself, your opinions and experiences. Do not ask a question unless you intend to listen to the answer and inquire into its value. Try to recollect that you are a very small affair in the world, and that the people around do not value you at all and grieve not when you are absent. Your only true greatness lies in your inner true self and it is not desirous of obtaining the applause of others. If you will follow these directions for one week you will find they will take considerable effort, and you will begin to discover a part of the meaning of the saying, "Man, know thyself."

It is not necessary to be conscious of the progress one has made. Nor is the date in any sense an extinguisher, as some have styled it. In these days we are too prone to wish to know everything all at once, especially in relation to ourselves. It may be desirable and encouraging to be thus conscious, but it is not necessary. We make a good deal of progress in our inner, hidden life of which we are not at all conscious. We do not know of it until some later life. So in this case many may be quite beyond the obstacles and not be conscious of it. It is best to go on with duty, and to refrain from this trying to take stock and measuring of progress. All of our progress is in the inner nature, and not in the physical where lives the brain, and from which the present question comes. The apparent physical progress is evanescent. It is ended when the body dies, at which time, if the inner man has not been allowed to guide us, the natural record against us will be a cipher, or "failure." Now, as the great Adepts live in the plane of our inner nature, it must follow that they might be actively helping every one of us after the date referred to, and we, as physical brain men, not be conscious of it on this plane.

... I strongly advise you to give up all yoga practices, which in almost all cases have disastrous results unless guided by a competent teacher. The concussions and explosions in your head are evidences that you are in no fit condition to try yoga practices, for they result from lesions of the brain, *i.e.*, from the bursting of the very minute brain cells. I am glad you have written to me upon this matter, that I may have an opportunity of warning you. Also I advise you to discontinue concentration on the vital centres, which again may prove dangerous unless under the guidance of a teacher. You have learnt, to a certain degree, the power of concentration, and the greatest help will now come to you from concentration upon the Higher Self, and aspiration toward the Higher Self. Also if you will take some subject or sentence from the *Bhagavat Gîtâ*, and concentrate your mind upon that and meditate upon it, you will find much good result from it, and there is no danger in such concentration.

As to the question about the disintegration of the astral body and the length of time beforehand when it could be seen. My answer was not meant to be definite as to years, except that I gave a period of two years as a long one before the death of the physical body. There are cases — perhaps rare — in which five years before the death of the physical, a clairvoyant has seen the disintegration of the astral beginning. The idea intended to be conveyed is, that regardless of periods of time, if the man is going to die naturally (and that includes by disease), the corruption, disintegrating or breaking up of the astral body may be perceived by those who can see that way. Hence the question of years is not involved. Violent deaths are not included in this, because the astral in such cases does not disintegrate beforehand. And the way of seeing such a death in advance is by another method altogether. Death from old age — which is the natural close of a cycle — is included in the answer as to death by disease, which might be called the disease of inability to fight off the ordinary breaking up of the cohesive forces.

You cannot develop the third eye. It is too difficult, and until you have cleared up a good deal more on philosophy it would be useless, and a useless sacrifice is a crime of folly. But here is advice given by many Adepts: every day and as often as you can, and on going to sleep and as you wake, think, think, think, on the truth that you are not body, brain, or astral man, but that you are THAT, and "THAT" is the Supreme Soul. For by this practice you will gradually kill the false notion which lurks inside that the false is the true, and the true is the false. By persistence in this, by submitting your daily thoughts each night to the judgment of your Higher Self, you will at last gain light.

Now as to *The Voice of the Silence* and the cycles of woe (undergone by the Arhan who remains to help mankind) it is easy to understand. You must always remember when reading such things, that terms must be used that the reader will understand. Hence, speaking thus, it must be said that there are such cycles of woe — from our standpoint — just as the fact that I have no amusements but nothing but work in the T. S. seems a great penance to those who like their pleasures. I, on the contrary, take pleasure and peace in the "self-denial" as they call it. Therefore it must follow that he who enters the secret Path finds his peace and pleasure in endless work for ages for Humanity. But, of course, with his added sight and knowledge, he must always be seeing the miseries of men self-inflicted. The mistake you make is to give the person thus "sacrificed" the same small qualities and longings as we now have, whereas the wider sweep and power of soul make what we call sacrifice and woe seem something different. Is not this clear, then? If it were stated otherwise than as the *Voice* has it, you would find many making the vow and then breaking it; but he who makes the vow with the full idea of its misery will keep it.

. . . . If we can all accumulate a fund of good for all the others we will thus dissipate many clouds. The follies and the so-called sins of people are really things that are sure to come to nothing if we treat them right. We must not be so prone as the people of the day are, of whom we are some, to criticise others and forget the beam in our own eye. The *Bhagavad Gîtâ* and Jesus are right in that they both shew us how to do our own duty and not go into that of others. Every time we think that someone else has done wrong we should ask ourselves two questions:

(1) Am I the judge in this matter who is entitled to try this person?

(2) Am I any better in my way, do I or do I not offend in some other way just as much as they do in this?

This will settle the matter I think. And in . . . there ought to be no judgments and no criticism. If some offend then let us ask what is to be done, but only when the offence is against the whole. When an offence is against *us*, then let it go. This is thought by some to be "goody-goody," but I tell you the heart, the soul, and the bowels of compassion are of more consequence than intellectuality. The latter will take us all sure to hell if we let it govern only. Be sure of this and try as much as you can to spread the true spirit in all directions, or else not only will there be individual failure, but also the circle H. P. B. made as a nucleus for possible growth will die, rot, fail, and come to nothing.

———

It is not possible to evade the law of evolution, but that law need not always be carried out in *one* way. If the same result is produced it is enough. Hence in any one hour or minute the being attaining adeptship could pass through countless experiences *in effect*. But, as a fact, no one becomes an adept until he has in some previous time gone through the exact steps needed. If you and I, for instance, miss adeptship in this *Manvantara*, we will emerge again to take up the work at a corresponding point in the much higher development of the next, although then we may seem low down in the scale, viewing us from the standard then to prevail.

———

The law is this. No man can rush on and fail to escape the counter current, and in proportion as he rushes so will be the force of the current. All members who work hard come at last to the notice of the Lodge, and the moment they do so, the Black Lodge also takes notice, and hence questions arise, and we are tried in subtle ways that surpass sight, but are strong for the undoing of him who is not prepared by right thought and sacrifice to the higher nature for the fight. I tell you this. It may sound mysterious, but it is the truth, and at this time we are all bound to feel the forces at work, for as we grow, so the other side gets ready to oppose.

———

. . . Be sure that you understand me right about the Black side. I mean this: that when men work along a good while, and really raise themselves up by that, they get the attention of the Black if they are of sufficient importance for it. I have their attention, and it makes a trouble now and then. What we all want to have, then, is the best armour for such a fight, and that is patience. Patience is a great thing, and will work in more ways than one, not only in personal life, but in wider concerns.

———

The difficulty of remembering the things you read, and the like, may be due to one or many causes. First, it indicates the need of mental discipline in the way of compelling yourself to serious reading and thinking, even though for a short time each day. If persisted in, this will gradually change the mental action, just as one can alter the taste for different sorts of food taken into the body. Again, if you have been dealing in what is known as Mind Cure or Metaphysical Healing, you should avoid it, because it will increase the difficulty you mention. It is different from good, ordinary, mental discipline. And also if you have been in any way following Spiritualism or indulging in psychic thoughts or visions or experiences, these would be a cause for the trouble, and should be abandoned.

There is no need for you to be a despairer. Reflect on that old verse, "What room is there for sorrow and what room for doubt in him who knows that the Self is one, and that all things are the Self, only differing in degree." This is a free rendering but is what it means. Now, it is true that a man cannot force himself at once into a new will and into a new belief but by thinking much on the same thing — such as this — he soon gets a new will and a new belief, and from it will come strength and also light. Try this plan. It is purely occult, simple, and powerful. I hope all will be well, and that as we are shaken up from time to time we shall grow strong.

———'s article strove to show that H. P. B. did not teach the doctrine of reincarnation in '77 as she did later, which is quite true so far as the public was then concerned, but she did to me and others teach it then as now, and further it seems clear what she meant, to wit, that there is no reincarnation for the astral monad, which is the astral man; and it being a theosophical doctrine that the astral man does not reincarnate save in exceptional cases, she taught then the same thing as she did later. Personally H. P. B. told me many times of the real doctrine of reincarnation, enforced by the case of the death of my own child, so I know what she thought and believed.

I am not able to give you the definition which you asked for, as it seems to me spirit cannot be defined except in this way, that the whole universe is made of spirit and matter, both constituting together the Absolute. What is not in matter is spirit, and what is not in spirit is matter; but there is no particle of matter without spirit, and no particle of spirit without matter. If this attempted definition is correct, you will see that it is impossible to define the things of the spirit, and that has always been said by the great teachers of the past.

———

What a petty lot of matter we spend time on, when so much is transitory. After a hundred years what will be the use of all this? Better that a hundred years hence a principle of freedom and an impulse of work should have been established. The small errors of a life are nothing, but the general sum of thought is much. . . . I care everything for the unsectarianism that H. P. B. died to start, and now threatened in its own house. Is it not true that Masters have forbidden Their chelas to tell under what orders they act for fear of the black shadow that follows innovations? Yes. . . .

———

Am very sorry to hear that your health is not good. In reply to your question: A sound body is not expected, because our race is unsound everywhere. It is Karma. Of course a correct mental and moral position will at last bring a sound body, but the process may, and often does, involve sickness. Hence sickness may be a blessing on two planes: (1) the mental and moral by opening the nature, and (2) on the physical as being the discharge into this plane of an inner sickness of the inner being.

———

The question of sex is not the most difficult. The personal one is still harder. I mean the purely personal, that relating to "me." The sexual relates really only to a low plane gratification. If Nature can beat you there, then she need not try the other, and *vice versa;* if she fails on the personal she may attempt the other, but then with small chance of success.

———

We all differ and must agree to disagree, for it is only by balancing contrary things that equilibrium (harmony) is obtained. Harmony does not come through likeness. If people will only let each other alone and go about their own business quietly all will be well. . . . It is one's duty to try and find one's own duty and not to get into the duty of another. And in this it is of the highest importance that we should detach our *minds* (as well as our tongues) from the duties and acts of others whenever those are outside of our own. If you can find this fine line of action and inaction you will have made great progress.

———

Do not stop to consider your progress at all, because that is the way to stop it; but take your mind off the question of your progress and do the best you can. I hope you will be able to acquire in no long time that frame of mind which you so much desire. I think you will acquire that if you will take your mind off yourself as much as possible, and throw it into something for someone else, which would, in course of time, destroy the self impression.

———

I regret exceedingly all your troubles and difficulties. They are all, it goes without saying, matters of Karma, and must right themselves in process of time. Meantime, your work and duty lies in continuing patient and persevering throughout. The troubles of your friends and relatives are not your Karma, though intimately associated with it by reason of the very friendship and relation. In the lives of all who aspire to higher things there is a more or less rapid precipitation of old Karma, and it is this which is affecting you. It will go off shortly, and you will have gained greatly in having gotten rid of a troublesome piece of business.

As it will take many a life for one to overcome the personal nature, there is no good in imagining what things and thoughts would then be like. It is certain that, in that long journey, the whole nature changing, it is adjusted to all conditions. Many of those matters which we call the woes of others are really nothing at all, and only "skin deep"; the real woe of the race is not that.

By setting apart a *particular* time for meditation a habit is formed, and as the time comes round the mind will, after a while, become trained, so that meditation at the particular time will become natural. Hence, as far as possible, it will be well for you to keep to the same hour.

You ask if I was at ——— where you saw me. Let me tell you something in confidence. I am around at all places, but, of course, most at such as where you . . . and others like that are, but it is not necessary for me to remember it at all, as it is done without that since this brain has enough to do here. To remember I should have to retire and devote myself to that, and it would make things no better.

A college course is not necessary for occultism. One of the best occultists I know was never in college. But if a man adds good learning to intuition and high aspiration he is naturally better off than another. I am constantly in the habit of consulting the dictionary and of thinking out the meanings and the correlations of words. Do the same. It is good.

The old mission of the Rosicrucians, though dead on the outside, is not dead, for the Masters were in that as They are in this, and it may be possible to usher in a new era of western occultism devoid of folly. We should all be ready for that if it be possible.

In regard to the pictures which you see, observe them with indifference, relying always on the Higher Self, and looking to it for knowledge and light, pictures or no pictures.

XXVII

On Work

Yes, that business is already a "back number," stale and unprofitable. I have found that work tells. While others fume and fret and sleep, and now and then start up to criticise, if you go right on and work, and let time, the great devourer, do the other work, you will see that in a little while that others will wake up once more to find themselves "left," as they say in the land of slang. Do, then, that way. Your own duty is hard enough to find out, and by attending to that you gain, no matter how small the duty may be. The duty of another is full of danger. May you have the light to see and to do! Tell ——— to work to the end to make himself an instrument for good work. Times change, men go here and there, and places need to be filled by those who can do the best sort of work and who are full of the fire of devotion and who have the right basis and a sure and solid one for themselves. My love to all.

I am very sorry that so many efforts on your part to influence the public press have been unsuccessful, but I feel sure that you will ultimately be successful. I am inclined to think that you will almost certainly find that articles written by Theosophists on the spot will obtain more ready admission than if you send them articles which have already been printed.

They have a more local colouring, and therefore a greater local interest. . . . I feel sure that by persistent and steady work, such as you are doing, you will win your way, and that even the most conservative papers will find it to their interest to insert articles.

Both ——— and ——— are two weak, half-corroded spots. It is due to (a) gossip about others, including me and others in the three lands; (b) to the personal element; (c) most of all to the absence of real faith in the Masters, for wherever that is not strong the work goes down; (d) to a sort of fear of public opinion; (e) to incomplete grasp of the elementary truths; and so on.

Stick to it that the way is to do all you can and let the results go. You have nothing to do with results; the other side will look out for that. This is really the culmination of the work of ages, and it would be a poor thing, indeed, if the Lodge had to depend alone on our puny efforts. Hence, go on and keep the spirit that you have only to proceed, and leave the rest to time and the Lodge. If all the other members had the same idea, it would be better for the old T. S. But let us hope on, for we have some any way, and that is more than none.

You are right, too, about *The Secret Doctrine*, it is a mine, and is the magazine for the warrior Theosophists, which is the description of you and me and some others.

Let us all be as silent as we may be, and work, work; for as the enemy rages, they waste time, while work shines forth after all is over, and we will see that as they fought we were building. Let that be our watchword .... I hope no weak souls will be shaken off their base. If they get on their *own* base they will not be shaken off.

XXVIII

On Wisdom in Action

This is the right conclusion, to let all talk and other people's concerns slip by and not meddle. No one should be taking information to another, for it fans a flame, and now we have to ignore everything and just work on, be good and kind and, like St. Paul's charity, overlook all things. Retire into your own silence and let all others be in the hands of Karma, as we all are. "Karma takes care of its own." It is better to have no side, for it is all for the Master and He will look out for all if each does just right, even if, to their view, another seems not to do so. By our not looking at their errors too closely the Master will be able to clear it all off and make it work well. The plan of quiet passive resistance, or rather, laying under the wind, is good and ought to work in all attacks. Retreat within your own heart and there keep firmly still. Resist without resisting. It is possible and should be attained. Once more, *au revoir* only, no matter what may happen, even irresistible Death itself. Earthquakes here yesterday: these signify some souls of use have come into the world somewhere; but where?

Well, now, just at this minute I do not know exactly what to say. Why not take up an easy and fluidic position in the matter? An occultist is never fixed to any particular mortal plan. Wait. All things come to him who waits in the right way. Make yourself in every way as good an instrument for any sort of work as you can. Every little thing I ever learned I have now found out to be of use to me in this work of ours. Ease of manner and of speech are of the best to have. Ease of mind and confidence are better than all in this work of dealing with other men — that is, with the human heart. The more wise one is the better he can help his fellows, and the more cosmopolitan he is the better, too. . . . When the hour strikes it will then find you ready; no man knows when the hour will strike. But he has to be ready. You see Jesus was in fact an occultist, and in the parable of the foolish virgins gave a real occult ordinance. It is a good one to follow. Nothing is gained, but a good deal is lost by impatience — not only strength, but also sight and intuition. So decide nothing hastily. Wait; make no set plan. Wait for the hour to make the decision, for if you decide in advance of the time you tend to raise a confusion. So have courage, patience, hope, faith, and cheerfulness.

The very first step towards being positive and self-centred is in the cheerful performance of duty. Try to take pleasure in doing what is your duty, and especially in the *little* duties of life. When doing any duty put your whole heart into it. There is much in this life that is bright if we would open our eyes to it. If we recognise this then we can bear the troubles that come to us calmly and patiently, for we know that they will pass away.

 . . . . You can solidify your character by attending to small things. By attacking small faults, and on every small occasion, one by one. This will arouse the inner attitude of attention and caution. The small faults and small occasions being conquered, the character grows strong. Feelings and desires are not wholly of the body. If the *mind* is deliberately taken off such subjects and placed on other and better ones, then the whole body will follow the mind and grow tractable. This struggle must be kept up, and after awhile it will be easier. Old age only makes this difference — the machine of body is less strong; for in old age the thoughts are the same if we let them grow without pruning.

There is never any need to worry. The good law looks out for all things, and all we have to do is our duty as it comes along from day to day. Nothing is gained by worrying about matters and about the way people do not respond. In the first place you do not alter people, and in the second, by being anxious as to things, you put an occult obstacle in the way of what you want done. It is better to acquire a lot of what is called carelessness by the world, but is in reality a calm reliance on the law, and a doing of one's own duty, satisfied that the results must be right, no matter what they may be. Think that over, and try to make it a part of your inner mind that it is no use to worry; that things will be all right, no matter what comes, and that you are resolved to do what you see before you, and trust to Karma for all the rest.

I am sorry to hear that you are passing through what you mention. Yet you knew it would have to come, and one learns, and the purpose of life is to learn. It is all made up of learning. So though it is hard it is well to accept it as you say.

Do you know what it is to resist without resistance?

That means, among other things, that too great an expenditure of strength, of "fortitude," is not wise. If one fights one is drawn into the swirl of events and thoughts instead of leaning back on the great ocean of the Self which is never moved. Now you see that, so lean back and look on at the ebb and flow of life that washes to our feet and away again many things that are not easy to lose or pleasant to welcome. Yet they all belong to Life, to the Self. The wise man has no personal possessions.

Anyway you are right that struggling is wrong. Do it quietly, that is the way the Masters do it. The reaction the other way is just as you say, but the Master has so much wisdom He is seldom if ever, the prey of reactions. That is why He goes slowly. But it is sure . . . I know how the cloud comes and goes. That is all right; just wait, as the song says, till they roll by.

Arouse, arouse in you the meaning of "Thou art That." Thou art the Self. This is the thing to think of in meditation, and if you believe it then tell others the same. You have read it before, but now try to realise it more and more each day and you will have the light you want. . . . If you will look for wisdom you will get it sure, and that is all you want or need. Am glad all looks well. It would always look well if each and all minded their own things and kept the mind free from all else.

Patience is really the best and most important thing, for it includes many. You cannot have it if you are not calm and ready for the emergency, and as calmness is the one thing necessary for the spirit to be heard, it is evident how important patience is. It also prevents one from precipitating a thing, for by precipitation we may smash a good egg or a good plan, and throw the Karma, for the time, off and prevent certain good effects flowing. So, keep right on and try for patience in all the very smallest things of life every day, and you will find it growing very soon, and with it will come greater strength and influence on and for others, as well as greater and clearer help from the inner side of things.

For the love of heaven do not take any tales or informations from any person to any other. The man who brought news to the king was sometimes killed. The surest way to make trouble out of nothing is to tell about it from one to another. Construe the words of the *Gîtâ* about one's own duty to mean that you have nothing to do in the smallest particular with other people's fancies, tales, facts, or other matters, as you will have enough to do to look out for your own duty. . . . Too much, too much, trying to force harmony. Harmony comes from a balancing of diversities, and discord from any effort to make harmony by force. . . . In all such things I never meddle, but say to myself it is none of my affair at all, and wait till it *comes to me* — and thank God if it never arrives! And that is a good rule for you.

Think of these points:

(a) Criticism should be abandoned. It is no good. Co-operation is better than criticism. The duty of another is dangerous for one whose duty it is not. The insidious coming of unbrotherly criticism should be warned against, prevented, stopped. By example you can do much, as also by word in due season.

(b) Calmness is now a thing to be had, to be preserved. No irritation should be let dwell inside. It is a deadly foe. Sit on all the small occasions that evoke it and the greater ones will never arise to trouble you.

(c) Solidarity.

(d) Acceptation of others.

It is not wise to be always analysing our faults and failures; to regret is waste of energy: if we endeavour to use all our energy in the service of the Cause, we shall find ourselves rising above our faults and failures, and though these must perhaps occur, they will lose their power to drag us down. Of course we do have to face our faults and fight them, but our strength for such a struggle will increase with our devotion and unselfishness. This does not mean that vigilance over one's thoughts and acts is ever to be relaxed.

If you will rely upon the truth that your inner self is a part of the great Spirit, you will be able to conquer these things that annoy, and if you will add to that a proper care of your bodily health, you will get strength in every department. Do not look at things as failures, but regard every apparent failure after real effort as a success, for the real test is in the effort and motive, and not in the result. If you will think over this idea on the lines of *The Bhagavat Gîtâ* you will gain strength from it.

As before so now I will do all I can for you, which is not much, as each must do for himself. Just stay loyal and true, and look for the indications of your own duty from day to day, not meddling with others, and you will find the road easier. It is better to die in one's own duty than to do that of another, no matter how well you do it. Look for peace that comes from a realisation of the true unity of all and the littleness of oneself. Give up in mind and heart all to the Self and you will find peace.

The deadening dullness you speak of is one of the trials of the age, but we have some good and earnest people, and they may act as the righteous men in the cities of old, for our ideas are more mighty than all the materialism of the age, which is sure to die out and be replaced by the truth. You will have to take care that the spirit of the time, and the wickedness and apathy of the people, do not engender in you a bitter spirit. This is always to be found in the beginning, but now, being forewarned, you are forearmed.

Do not allow bitterness to come up; keep off all personalities all the time; let the fight be for a cause and not against anyone. Let no stones be thrown. Be charitable. Do not let people be asked to step out, no matter what they do;

when they want to go they may go, but don't have threats nor discipline, it does no good but a lot of harm.

Say, look here, never growl at anything you have to do. If you have to go, just take it as a good thing you have to do, and then it will redound to the good of them and yourself, but if it is a constant cross then it does no good and you get nothing. Apply your theories thus. . . . It is a contest of smiles if we really know our business. . . . Never be afraid, never be sorry, and cut all doubts with the sword of knowledge.

I think that you will be helped if you will try to aid some poor, distressed person by merely talking and expressing your sympathy if you are not able to help in money, though the very fact of giving five cents to someone who needs it is an act which, if done in the right spirit, that of true brotherliness, will help the one who gives. I suggest this because you will, by doing so, set up fresh bonds of sympathy between you and others, and by trying to alleviate the sorrows or sufferings of others, you will find strength come to you when you most need it.

Let them croak, and if we keep silent it will have no effect and as there has been trouble enough it is better not to make it any worse by referring to it. The only strength it has is when we take notice. It is better policy for all of us who are in earnest and united to keep still in any matter that has any personal bearing.

Silentio, my dear, is almost as good as patience. He laughs best who does it last, and time is a devil for grinding things. . . . Use the time in getting calmness and solid strength, for a deep river is not so because it has a deep bed, but because it has *volume*.

Rely within yourself on your Higher Self always, and that gives strength, as the Self uses whom it will. Persevere, and little by little *new ideals* and thought-forms will drive out of you the old ones. This is the eternal process.

Troubles are ahead, of course, but I rather think that the old war-horse of the past will not be easily frightened or prevented from the road. Do your best to make and keep good thought and feeling of solidarity. . . . Our old lion of the Punjab is not so far off, but all the same is not in the place some think, or in the condition either.

The way gets clearer as we go on, but as *we* get clearer we get less anxious as to the way ahead.

There is service objective and its counterpart within, which being stronger will at last manifest without.

Do not judge in anger, for though the anger passes the judgment remains.

The promises I made to myself are just as binding as any others.

Be true lovers, but of God, and not of each other. Love each the other in that to one another ye mirror God, for that God is in you each.

We all are; I too. We never *were* anything, but only continually are. What we are now determines what we will be.

———

In order to off-set the terribly cold effect of perceiving the littleness of human affairs, one must inculcate in oneself a great compassion which will include oneself also. If this is not done, contempt comes on, and the result is dry, cold, hard, repellent and obstructive to all good work.

———

I know that his absence is a loss to you, but I think if you will regard all things and events as being in the Self and It in them, making yourself a part of the whole, you will see there is no real cause for sorrow or fear. Try to realise this and thus go in confidence and even joy.

———

There are valleys in which the greatest shadows are due to old lives in other bodies, and yet the intensity of universal love and of aspiration will dissipate those in an instant of time.

An Occult Novel

A TIRELESS worker, Mr. Judge, was always proposing new modes of activity. One never knew what fresh idea would not emanate from his indefatigable mind. One idea with which he occupied some of his lighter moments, was that of an occult novel. It was his idea that a friend of his should write this, from incidents and materials to be furnished by himself, and to this idea he adhered, even having the title copyrighted, with the name of his author, despite the laughing protests of this friend, to whose outcries and statements that she never could, and never should, write a novel, Mr. Judge would smilingly reply: "Oh, yes! You will do it when the time comes." From time to time he sent to this friend suggestions, incidents and other material for this novel, the same being on odds and ends of paper, often rough wrapping paper, and being jotted down under a lamp-post at night while he waited for his tram, or in court while he waited for the case in which he was engaged to come up. On these scraps are also marginal notes, as he accepted or rejected the ideas of his own prolific mind. These notes are given here as such. It has been suggested that the recipient of these materials should still write the novel as proposed, but setting aside the fact that she could not be sure of properly rendering the real ideas of Mr. Judge, it is also thought that readers will much prefer to have the notes precisely as Mr. Judge set them down.

The printed title-page runs as follows:

IN A BORROWED BODY.
The Journey of a Soul.
BY
J. Campbell Ver-Planck, F. T. S.
1891.

The name is filled in in the writing of Mr. Judge, and there is this marginal note. "Copyright gone to Washngn."

(All "Notes" are to be understood as being marginal ones made by Mr. Judge unless otherwise stated.)

Memo. about *Borrowed Body*

The point on which it should all turn is not so much reincarnation as the use of a borrowed body, which is a different kind of reincarnation from that of Arnold's *Phra the Phoenician.*

This will also give chance to show the other two sorts of reincarnation, *e.g.:* —

(a) Ordinary reincarnation in which there is no memory of the old personality, as the astral body is new; and:

(b) Exception as to astral body; but similarity of conception to that of ordinary cases, where the child retains the old astral body and hence memory of old personality and acquaintance with old knowledge and dexterity.

A Chapter
The Assembling of the Skandhas

On the death of body the Kama principle collects the Skandhas in space, or at the rebirth of the Ego the Skandhas rush together and assemble about it to go with it in the new life.

Another

The Unveiling of the Sun

There is the real and unreal sun. The real one is hidden by a golden vase, and the devotee prays:

"Unveil, O Pushan, the true Sun's face," etc. A voice (or other) says "thou art that vase" and then he knows that he alone hides the true Sun from himself.

Pushan is the guide and watches on the path to the Sun.

The eulogy of the Sun and the Soul are enshrined in a golden rose or lotus in the heart which is impregnable.

The theme of the book is not always teacher and pupil.

He first strives for some lives ordinarily and then in one he grows old and wise, and sitting before a temple one day in Madura he dies slowly, and like a dissolving view he sees the adepts around him aiding him; also a small child which seems to be himself, and then thick darkness. He is born then in the usual way.

Twice this is repeated, each time going through the womb but with the same astral body.

Then he lives the third life to forty-nine, and comes again to die and with the same aid he selects a foreign child who is dying.

Child dying. Skandhas collecting, child's Ego going — left, spark of life low: relatives about bed.

He enters by the way the mind went out and revivifies the body. Recovery, youth, etc., etc.

This is his borrowed body.

Memo. No. 2

A couple of Incidents for the Book

A round tower used by the fire worshippers in Ireland

and other isles in early ages. A temple is attached to it; quaint structure — one priest and one neophyte.

People below the tower coming into the temple grounds as the religion is in its decadence.

On the top of the tower is the neophyte, who in the face of the prevailing scepticism clings to the dead faith and to the great priest. His duty is to keep a fire on the tower burning with aromatic woods. He leans over the fire; it burns badly; the wood seems green; he blows it up; it burns slightly; he hears the voices of the disputers and sellers below; goes to the tower and gazes over while the fire goes slowly out. He is a young man of singular expression, not beautiful but powerful face; intense eyes, long dark hair, and far gazing eyes of a greyish colour unusual for such hair. Skin clear with a shifting light flowing from it. Sensitive face; blushes easily but now and then stern. As he still gazes the fire goes out. Just then a tall old man comes up the stairs and stands upon the tower top at opposite side, looking at the fire and then at the young man and withdraws not his gaze for an instant. It is a sternly powerful drawing look. He is very tall, dark brown eyes, grey hair, long beard. The young man feels his look and turns about and sees the fire out completely, while its last small cloud of smoke is floating off beyond the tower. They look at each other. In the young's man face you see the desperate first impulse to excuse, and then the sudden thought that excuses are useless because childish, for he knew his duty — to keep the small spiral of smoke ever connecting heaven with earth, in the hope, however vain, that thus the old age might be charmed to return. The old man raises his hand, points away from the tower and says "go." Young man descends.

II. *A battle.* — In the hottest a young soldier armed to the teeth, fighting as if it made no matter whether he win or lose, die or live. Strange weapons, sounds and clouds.

Wounded, blood flowing. It is the young man of the tower. He sinks down taken prisoner. In a cell, condemned, for they fear his spiritual power. Conflict between the last remnant of the old religion and the new, selfish faith.

Taken to his execution. Two executioners. They bind him standing and stand behind and at side; each holds a long straight weapon with a curved blunt blade, curved to (fit?) about the neck. They stand at opposite sides, place those curved blunt blades holding his neck like two crooks. They pull — a sickening sound: his head violently pulled out close to the shoulder leaves a jagged edge. The body sways and falls. It was the way they made such a violent exit for a noble soul as they thought would keep it bound in the astral earth sphere for ages.

III. That young man again. He approaches an old man (of the tower). Young one holds parchments and flowers in his hand, points to parchments and asks explanation. Old one says, "Not now; when I come again I will tell you."

Note. — Keep this, Julius.   W. Q. J.
                                Z. L. Z.

The next batch of notes is headed by the single word: "*Book.*" Then follow four lines of shorthand. After these the words:

"Incidents showing by picture his life in other ages; the towers; the battle; the death; the search for knowledge and the sentiment expressed in the flowers."

Eusebio Rodrigues de Undiano was a notary in Spain who found among the effects of his father many old parchments written in a language which was unknown to him. He discovered it was Arabic, and in order to decipher them learned that tongue. They contained the story.

Note. — No initiates; Lytton only.

Eusebio de Undiano is only one of the old comrades reborn in Spain who searches like Nicodemus for the light.

Note. — Yes.

Eusebio de Undiano finds in his father's parchments confirmation of what the possession of the body has often told him.

Note. — Yes.

This person in the body never gave his name to anyone and has no name.

An autobiographical story? No? *Yes!* Related by one who was struck; by an admirer who suspected something? No; because that is hearsay evidence; the proof is incomplete, whereas he relating it himself is either true, or a mere insane fancy. It is better to be insane than be another's tool.

Stick to the tower and the head-chopping business. Let him be that young man and after the head loss he wanders in Kama Loca and there he sees the old man who was killed on the tower soon after the fire went out. The old man tells him that he will tell all when they return to earth.

He wanders about the tower vicinity seeking a birth, until one day he sees vague shapes suddenly appearing and disappearing. They are not dressed like his countrymen down below on the earth. This goes on. They seem friendly and familiar, the one requesting him to go with them, he refuses. They are more powerful than he is yet they do not compel him but show him their power. One day one was talking to him; he again refuses unless something might show him that he ought to go. Just then he hears a bell sound, such as he never heard before. It vibrates through him and seems to open up vistas of the strange past, and in a moment he consents to go.

They reach Southern India and there he sees the old man of the tower, whom he addresses, and again asks the burning question about the parchment. The old man says again the same as before and adds that he had better come again into the world in that place.

The darkness and silence. The clear, hot day. The absence of rain. After listening to the old man he consents inwardly to assume life there and soon a heavy storm arises, the rain beats, he feels himself carried to the earth and in deep darkness. A resounding noise about him. It is the noise of the growing plants. This is a rice field with some sesamum in it. The moisture descends and causes the expanding; sees around, all is motion and life. Inclosed in the sphere of some rice, he bemoans his fate. He is born in a Brahmin's house.

Note. — Shall the question of reincarnation through cloud and rain and seed and thus from the seed of the man, be gone into?

He is the young man. He knows much. He dies at nineteen. Strange forms around his bed who hold him. They carry him back to the land of the towers. He recognises it again and sees that ages have passed since the fire went out, and in the air he perceives strange shapes and sees incessantly a hand as of Fate, pointing to that Island. The towers are gone, the temples and the monuments. All is altered. They take him to a populous city and as he approaches he sees over one house a great commotion in the air. Shapes moving. Bright flashes, and puffs as of smoke. They enter the room, and on the bed is the form of a young boy given up to die, with relatives weeping. His guides ask him if he will borrow that body about to be deserted and use it for the good of their Lodge. He consents. They warn him of the risks and dangers.

The boy's breathing ceases and his eyes close, and a bright flash is seen to go off from it (the body). He sees the blood slowing down. THEY push him, and he feels dark again. Boy revives. Physician takes hope. "Yes; he will recover, with care." He recovers easily. Change in his character. Feels strange in his surroundings, etc.

The place in India where he went after death which was again sudden (how?). A large white building. Gleaming marble. Steps. Pillars. A hole that has yellowish glow that looks like water. Instruction as to the work to be done, and the journey to the land of the tower, in search of a body to borrow. As to bodies being deserted by the tenant that might live if well understood and well connected with a new soul. The difference between such a birth and an ordinary birth where the soul really owns the body, and between those bodies of insane people which are not deserted, but where the owner really lives outside. Bodies of insane are not used because the machine itself is out of order, and would be useless to the soul of a sane person.

Note. — Julius; keep these. I will send them now and then. But before you go away, return to me so I can keep the run of it. May change the scheme. The motive is in the title I gave you.

Note. — No one who has not consciously lived the double life of a man who is in the use and possession of a body not his own can know the agony that so often falls to one in such a case. I am not the original owner of this body that I now use. It was made for another, and for some little time used by him, but in the storm of sickness he left it here to be buried, and it would have been laid away in the earth if I had not taken it up, vivified its failing energies and carried it through some years of trial by sickness and accident. But the first owner had not been in it long enough to sow any troublesome seeds of disease; he left a heritage of good family blood and wonderful endurance. That he should have left this form so well adapted for living, at least seems inconceivable, unless it was that he could not use it, sick or well, for any of his own purposes. At any rate it is mine now, but while at first I thought it quite an acquisition there are often times when I wish I had not thus taken another man's frame, but had come into life in the ordinary way.

A Couple of Incidents for The Book

Incident of the letter and picture.

There was a very curious old man (sufficient description to add).

Sent a small cardboard in which was a picture, a head, and over it appeared to be placed a thin sheet of paper, gummed over the sides to the back. He asked if I could tell him anything of the picture which was visible through the thin paper. Having great curiosity, I lifted up the thin paper, and at once there seemed to be printed off from its underside a red circle surrounding the head on the board. In one instance this circle turned black and so did the entire inside space including the head which was then obliterated. In the other the red circle seemed to get on fire inward, and then the whole included portion burned up. On examining the thin paper on underside there were traces of a circle, as if with paste.

He laughed and said that curiosity was not always rewarded.

Took it to several chemists in Paris, who said that they

knew of no substance that would do this. The old chemist in Ireland said a very destructive thing called Fluorine might be liberated thus and do it, but that it was only a thing with chemists and analysts.

(*Note by the compiler.* — In his travels Mr. Judge met many strange people and saw some extraordinary sights. Now and again he would tell one of these to be included in the novel, but just in this unfinished and vague way. When asked to tell more, he would smile and shake his head, saying: "No, No; little brothers must finish it.")

Another Incident

The temple on the site of the present city of Conjeveram was about to be consecrated and the regular priests were all ready for the ceremony. Minor ceremonies had taken place at the laying of the corner-stone, but this was to exceed that occasion in importance. A large body of worshippers were gathered not for the gratification of curiosity, but in order to receive the spiritual benefits of the occasion and they filled the edifice so that I could not get inside. I was thus compelled to stand just at the edge of the door, and that was, as I afterwards found out, the best place I could have selected if I had known in advance what was to take place. A few days before a large number of wandering ascetics had arrived and camped on a spot near the temple, but no one thought much of it because used to seeing such people. There was nothing unnatural about these men, and all that could be said was that a sort of mysterious air hung about them, and one or two children declared that on one evening none of the visitors could be found at their camp nor any evidence that men had been there, but they were not believed, because the ascetics were there as usual the next morning. Two old men in the city said that the visitors were Devas in their "illusionary form," but there was too much excitement about the dedication to allow much thought on the subject. The event, however, proved the old men right.

At the moment when the people in the temple were expecting the priests to arrive, the entire body of ascetics appeared at the door with a wonderful looking sage like man at their head, and they entered the edifice in the usual formal way of the priests and the latter on arriving made no disturbance, but took what places they could, simply saying: "they are the Devas." The strangers went on with the ceremonies, and all the while a light filled the building and music from the air floated over the awestruck worshippers.

When the time came for them to go they all followed the leader in silence to the door. I could see inside, and as I was at the door could also see outside. All the ascetics came to the entrance but not one was seen to go beyond it, and none were ever perceived by any man in the city again. They melted away at the threshold. It was their last appearance, for the shadow of the dark age was upon the people, preventing such sights for the future. The occurrence was the topic of conversation for years, and it was all recorded in the archives of the city.

In a Borrowed Body

I MUST tell you first what happened to me in this present life since it is in this one that I am relating to you about many other lives of mine.

I was a simple student of our high Philosophy for many lives on earth in various countries, and then at last developed in myself a desire for action. So I died once more as so often before and was again reborn in the family of a Rajah, and in time came to sit on his throne after his death.

Two years after that sad event one day an old wandering Brahmin came to me and asked if I was ready to follow my vows of long lives before, and go to do some work for my old master in a foreign land. Thinking this meant a journey only I said I was.

"Yes," said he, "but it is not only a journey. It will cause you to be here and there all days and years. Today here, tonight there."

"Well," I replied, "I will do even that, for my vows had no conditions and master orders."

I knew of the order, for the old Brahmin gave me the sign marked on my forehead. He had taken my hand, and covering it with his waist-cloth, traced the sign in my palm under the cloth so that it stood out in lines of light before my eyes.

He went away with no other word, as you know they so often do, leaving me in my palace. I fell asleep in the heat, with only faithful Gopal beside me. I dreamed and thought I was at the bedside of a mere child, a boy, in a foreign land unfamiliar to me only that the people looked like what I knew of the Europeans. The boy was lying as if dying, and relatives were all about the bed.

A strange and irresistible feeling drew me nearer to the child, and for a moment I felt in this dream as if I were about to lose consciousness. With a start I awoke in my own palace — on the mat where I had fallen asleep, with no one but Gopal near and no noise but the howling of jackals near the edge of the compound.

"Gopal," I said, "how long have I slept?"

"Five hours, master, since an old Brahmin went away, and the night is nearly gone, master."

I was about to ask him something else when again sleepiness fell upon my senses, and once more I dreamed of the small dying foreign child.

The scene had changed a little, other people had come in, there was a doctor there, and the boy looked to me, dreaming so vividly, as if dead. The people were weeping, and his mother knelt by the bedside. The doctor laid his head on the child's breast a moment. As for myself I was drawn again nearer to the body and thought surely the people were strange not to notice me at all. They acted as if no stranger were there, and I looked at my clothes and saw they were eastern and bizarre to them. A magnetic line seemed to pull me to the form of the child.

And now beside me I saw the old Brahmin standing. He smiled.

"This is the child," he said, "and here must you fulfil a part of your vows. Quick now! There is no time to lose, the child is almost dead. These people think him already a corpse. You see the doctor has told them the fatal words, 'he is dead!' "

Yes, they were weeping. But the old Brahmin put his hands on my head, and submitting to his touch, I felt myself in my dream falling asleep. A dream in a dream. But I woke in my dream, but not on my mat with Gopal near me. I was that boy I thought. I looked out through his eyes, and near me I heard, as if his soul had slipped off to the ether with a sigh of relief. The doctor turned once more and I opened my eyes — his eyes — on him.

The physician started and turned pale. To another I heard him whisper "automatic nerve action." He drew near, and the intelligence in that eye startled him to paleness. He did not see the old Brahmin making passes over this body I was in and from which I felt great waves of heat and life rolling over me — or the boy.

And yet this all now seemed real as if my identity was merged in the boy.

I was that boy and still confused, vague dreams seemed to flit through my brain of some other plane where I thought I was again, and had a faithful servant named Gopal; but that must be dream, this the reality. For did I not see my mother and father, the old doctor and the nurse so long in our house with the children. Yes; of course this is the reality.

And then I feebly smiled, whereon the doctor said:

"Most marvellous. He has revived. He may live."

He was feeling the slow moving pulse and noting that breathing began and that vitality seemed once more to return to the child, but he did not see the old Brahmin in his illusionary body sending air currents of life over the body of this boy, who dreamed he had been a Rajah with a faithful servant named Gopal. Then in the dream sleep seemed to fall upon me. A sensation of falling, falling came to my brain, and with a start I awoke in my palace on my own mat. Turning to see if my servant was there I saw him standing as if full of sorrow or fear for me.

"Gopal, how long have I slept again?"

"It is just morning, master, and I feared you had gone to Yama's dominions and left your own Gopal behind."

No, I was not sleeping. This was reality, these my own dominions. So this day passed as all days had except that the dream of the small boy in a foreign land came to my mind all day until the night when I felt more drowsy than usual. Once more I slept and dreamed.

The same place and the same house, only now it was morning there. What a strange dream I thought I had had; as the doctor came in with my mother and bent over me, I heard him say softly:

"Yes, he will recover. The night sleep has done good.

Take him, when he can go, to the country, where he may see and walk on the grass."

As he spoke behind him I saw the form of a foreign looking man with a turban on. He looked like the pictures of Brahmins I saw in the books before I fell sick. Then I grew very vague and told my mother: "I had had two dreams for two nights, the same in each. I dreamed I was a king and had one faithful servant for whom I was sorry as I liked him very much, and it was only a dream, and both were gone."

My mother soothed me, and said: "Yes, yes, my dear."

And so that day went as days go with sick boys, and early in the evening I fell fast asleep as a boy in a foreign land, in my dream, but did no more dream of being a king, and as before I seemed to fall until I woke again on my mat in my own palace with Gopal sitting near. Before I could rise the old Brahmin, who had gone away, came in and I sent Gopal off.

"Rama," said he, "as boy you will not dream of being Rajah but now you must know that every night as sleeping king you are waking boy in foreign land. Do well your duty and fail not. It will be some years, but Time's never-stopping car rolls on. Remember my words," and then he passed through the open door.

So I knew those dreams about a sick foreign boy were not mere dreams but that they were recollections, and I condemned each night to animate that small child just risen from the grave, as his relations thought, but I knew that his mind for many years would not know itself, but would ever feel strange in its surroundings, for, indeed, that boy would be myself inside and him without, his friends not seeing that he had fled away and another taken his place. Each night I, as sleeping Rajah who had listened to the words of sages, would be an ignorant foreign boy, until through lapse of years and effort unremittingly continued I learned how to live two lives at once. Yet horrible at first seemed the thought that although my life in that foreign land as a growing youth would be undisturbed by vague dreams of independent power as Rajah, I would always, when I woke on my mat, have a clear remembrance of what at first seemed only dreams of being a king, with vivid knowledge that while my faithful servant watched my sleeping form I would be masquerading in a borrowed body, unruly as the wind. Thus as a boy I might be happy, but as a king miserable maybe. And then after I should become accustomed to this double life, perhaps my foreign mind and habits would so dominate the body of the boy that existence there would grow full of pain from the struggle with an environment wholly at war with the thinker within.

But a vow once made is to be fulfilled, and Father Time eats up all things and ever the centuries.

William Quan Judge

[Condensed from a four-part biographical sketch, originally published in *The Irish Theosophist*, vol. iv, 1896.]

WILLIAM QUAN JUDGE was born in Dublin, Ireland on April 13, 1851, son of Alice Mary Quan and Frederick H. Judge, a Mason and student of mysticism. Of William's childhood there is little to say except for a memorable illness in his seventh year. Shortly after the physician had declared the child dead it was discovered that he had revived. During convalescence he showed aptitudes and knowledge never before displayed. He seemed the same and yet not the same. Upon recovery he devoured every book he could obtain relating to Mesmerism, phrenology, character reading, religion, magic, Rosicrucianism, and the Book of Revelation. But the magnetic link so abruptly renewed in his near-mortal illness was perhaps never fully vitalized for he remained physically frail. His mother died at the birth of her seventh child, and when William was thirteen, the family moved to the United States, arriving in New York on July 14, 1864.

W. Q. Judge worked as a clerk before entering the law office of George P. Andrews, later a Justice of the Supreme Court of the State of New York. On coming of age, Judge became a naturalized citizen of the United States and in May 1872 was admitted to the bar of New York, specializing in commercial law. In 1874 he married Ella M. Smith of Brooklyn, by whom he had a daughter, whose death in early childhood was long a source of deep, though quiet, sorrow to them both.

At this time the tide of occult inquiry and speculation was high and the experiences of numbers of people at the "Eddy Homestead" in Vermont were attracting wide attention. A series of articles by H. S. Olcott appeared in the New York *Daily Graphic* (later published as *People from the Other World*), and Judge wrote to the author for further information. On learning of his interest, H. P. Blavatsky invited the young lawyer to call on her. Thereafter he spent much of his time with her and Colonel Olcott, studying under her direction. He was among those present at her rooms at 46 Irving Place, New York on the evening of September 7, 1875, when the proposal was made to form a society for research into the spiritual laws governing the physical universe. Judge was called to the chair and he nominated Olcott as chairman; he himself was nominated as secretary. This was the beginning of the Theosophical Society.

During the writing of *Isis Unveiled* — H. P. Blavatsky's first major theosophical work — Judge was one of those who assisted her and Colonel Olcott with the final preparation of the manuscript. The next year, in December 1878, H. P. Blavatsky and Olcott went to India, appointing Major-General Abner Doubleday president pro tem and W. Q. Judge recording secretary. They carried on the responsibilities of the Theosophical Society in America as best they could. Although the work went slowly at first, with little activity, the link was kept unbroken. Theirs was a difficult task indeed because H. P. Blavatsky, who was the one great exponent, had left the field, and the curiosity and interest excited by her original and striking mission had died down. Henceforth the Society was to subsist on its philosophical basis alone, and this principle Judge adhered to until his death, his energies being devoted to the dissemination of the theosophical philosophy and the practical realization of universal brotherhood.

In 1884, Judge joined H. P. Blavatsky in Paris, spending a few months with her before traveling to India; then, after a brief stay in Madras, he returned to America to pick up his professional and theosophical duties. Little by little he gathered about him a number of earnest seekers, and gradually built up a strong American section. From scoffing and jeering the press began to accept his articles on theosophy. In 1886 he founded and edited *The Path* magazine, started a printing press, and wrote unceasingly: books, articles, and letters to inquirers and members all over the country. He lectured from coast to coast, accomplishing the work of several men.

Finally, when the work had increased to large proportions, Judge relinquished his profession to give his entire time to the Society. However, as a result of continuous overwork and weakened by recurrent Chagres fever contracted in South America years earlier, his health gave way and, shortly before his 45th birthday, he died in New York on March 21, 1896.

So much for the outer facts of his life. As a mystic W.Q.J. had another office, simple yet profound, rarely visible on the surface, yet luminous. During the years 1887-8 he wrote to two friends a series of letters (later issued under the title *Letters That Have Helped Me*). It would be difficult to trace the lives touched, the many individuals for whom these letters have been as a light to the soul. Those who have worked with true devotion for the welfare of their brothers know well the uplifting, widening force which flowed through them, ripening the character, developing the higher nature, and letting patience have her perfect work. A friend to all men and women he was, yet impersonal always.

* * *

On page 68 of the first volume of *Letters* is a letter from an adept from which a certain portion ("private instruction") is omitted. That omitted portion runs as follows:

"Is the choice made? Then Y. will do well to see W. Q. J. and to acquaint him with this letter. For the first year or two no better guide can be had. For when the 'PRESENCE' is upon him, he knows well that which others only suspect and 'divine.' . . . . is useful to 'Path,' but greater services may be rendered to him, who, of all chelas, suffers most and demands, or even expects the least."

(If this extract be fitted into the original letter its immense importance in respect to W. Q. Judge may be realised by the intuitive student.)

Summing up his life, one must still say what was written soon after his departure: "In thinking of this helper and teacher of ours, I find myself thinking almost wholly of the future. He was one who never looked back; he looked forward always. . . . We think of him not as of a man departed from our midst, but as a soul set free to work its mighty mission, rejoicing in that freedom, resplendent in compassion and power. His was a nature that knew no trammels, but acknowledged the divine laws in all things. He was, as he himself said, 'rich in hope.' "

J. N.